SUCK LESS

WHERE THERE'S A WILLAM, THERE'S A WAY

GRAND CENTRAL
PUBLISHING

NEW YORK   BOSTON

Cover design by Brian Lemus
Cover photo by Mathu Andersen
Cover copyright © 2016 by Hachette Book Group, Inc.

Grand Central Publishing
Hachette Book Group
1290 Avenue of the Americas, New York, NY 10104
grandcentralpublishing.com
twitter.com/grandcentralpub

First Edition: October 2016

Grand Central Publishing is a division of Hachette Book Group, Inc. The Grand Central Publishing name and logo is a trademark of Hachette Book Group, Inc.

Print book interior design by Timothy Shaner, NightandDayDesign.biz.

Library of Congress Cataloging-in-Publication Data has been applied for.

ISBNs: 978-1-4555-6619-8 (trade paperback), 978-1-4555-6621-1 (ebook)

Printed in the United States of America

Q-MA

10 9 8 7 6 5 4

Possession is nine-tenths of ownership, so...

This book is dedicated to

_____

(Your Name Here)

*PS: Feel free to color me, and tag a bitch on Instagram @Willam.
And if it doesn't suck, I'll repost it. If you have a big enough
dick, just shove a Sharpie between your cock and balls,
and paint like those gifted elephants, who are like
an endangered species, too. I guess*

CONTENTS

by **NEIL PATRICK HARRIS**

Willam helped me win a Tony.

She probably goes around claiming she was solely responsible for my winning a Tony (and I'm not talking about Romo or Hawk or Danza or Shalhoub—as fun as that would be). She'd be lying (and not on her back, for once). But when I signed up to portray Hedwig on Broadway I knew that, considering I'd never donned drag once in my life, I'd need a bit of help.

Nay, I'd need a shit ton of help. I was (still am) a massive fan of *RuPaul's Drag Race* and marveled at the unbridled confidence and fearlessness of each season's girls, but there was one in particular whose brain I really wanted to pick, whose lessons I really wanted to learn. When Latrice Royale told me to fuck myself, I called Willam.

I kid. It was always Willam. She had me mesmerized from the first moment I saw her on screen. There is something absolutely undeniable about her charisma, wit, style, cuntiness, and beauty (not necessarily in that order). I needed to learn from the master—er, mistress.

And, gurrrrl, did she deliver. I truly couldn't have been a believable woman without her. She taught me how to sway my hips when I walk. How to work a wig. How to tape my junk to my taint. How to kneel like a lady. How to not have my eyes water when I was gagging. How to cut a prostitute enough to make him bleed and keep his mouth shut but not enough to make him bleed out and keep his eyes shut. Helpful stuff like that.

So if you're reading this book for tips, you're in great hands. They may be missing a fake nail or three and shaking from withdrawals, but the advice will be invaluable.

Willam rules.

Remember them.

N

" Hello, blood relatives, the black girls who work at TSA, homosexuals, and those fag-adjacent. "

"OHMYGOD, YOU'RE SO PRETTY!"

"HOW DO YOU WALK IN THOSE?"

"CAN I TOUCH YOUR HAIR?"

Those are three things I hear from strangers every time I go out. The answers are

"My home has mirrors, so I'm well aware."

"Christ's endless love."

"Please stop touching my hair," because no one actually waits for the answer before the petting zoo begins.

There's a special something a lot of drag queens (and the TSA ladies) have that average people don't. It's not a laptop in a bag or a lithium battery. It's a little something extra I call the Zeta Factor. Y'know Catherine Zeta-Jones, right? Oscar winner, trophy wife, bipolar beauty. Well, take away the Zeta and she's just ol' Cathy Jones. Ain't nobody wanna be no Cathy Jones.

The jungle got the fever from me.

To find a queen, just follow the trail:
1. *Cock ring/hair elastic*
2. *Ciggie butts*
3. *Duct tape*

No, thank you. Ya gotta throw some fuckin' Zeta into your life and make it sparkle.

So how does a typical person find their sparkle? Self-reflection in a Zen garden? Sure. That'll work fine, I bet. Although smart money says that if you're looking for some sparkle, it may be easier to just find a fucking drag queen. Drag queens, generally, make life better all around. Think of it this way: If you were bored at home and had my number in your phone, wouldn't you call it? Odds are, your night would be more entertaining. I do all the things you may think twice about before even thinking once. It's probably better that you don't do some of those things, but you could always learn from my mistakes or at least borrow my stuff while I'm in jail (page 102).

Now, remember: If you do happen to **clock**˙ a drag queen in her natural habitat, try to act naturally with no sudden movements (otherwise, she'll think you have coke). Approach the subject as you would approach any sort of domesticated mammal at, say, a Busch Gardens. The animal can touch you, but make no moves to disturb her/it. Touching a drag queen's hair, face, phone, or man is not advisable. For instance, if I'm in the room, you'll always have to keep in mind that any drink in the room belongs to me by default. Maybe your bag, too. Who knows? Maybe I'm

˙ If you see a **boldface term**, you can find its definition in the Dragtionary in the back (page 212).

lookin' for mints or something to suck on. You don't know my life. I probably just need it for a minute for my gig or to…well… it doesn't matter, really. This isn't about me (for once). It's about you and how you can *Suck Less* at a variety of things drag queens are so much better at than the average person. I've got clap backs and life hacks and tips on classing up a simple grab-and-run lifting spree to the much more dignified act of larceny. Super-important life stuff with my own special, secret fag-swag sauce. So welcome to Willam's School of Bitchcraft and Wiggotry. Class is in session.

FIND A DRAG QUEEN

I f you need more hands-on advice, please find one of my sisters in your own hood. Here are some places to find drag queens:

- ▥ **At the CVS**, *waiting in the razor aisle for an associate to take up more of her fuckin' day while opening up the lock on the plastic thing with Gillette Mach3 blades.*

- ▥ **Nightclubs** *on nights when the bar has nothing else going on so they do a drag show and some kinda two-dollar well drink special.*

- ▥ **The mall.** *Look for frowning faces in black. All those MAC and Sephora fags consider their day jobs contouring concentration camps.*

- ▥ **Their parents' house** *(before they move out and once they've moved back in).*

- ▥ **Farmers' markets.** *Why'd the vegan hooker go to the farmers' market? She was looking for whoreganic opportunities.*

No retouching—f'real!

THIS IS WHAT I LOOK LIKE

WITHOUT RETOUCHING

How to **SUCK LESS** at
MAKEUP

HOW TO MAKE A DRAG LOOK WORK IN EVERYDAY LIFE

In the right light and from across the street, you'd swear I was a real woman. The closer I get, the more apparent it is that I am one of those girls with some skirtsteak. I'm not into heavily painting my face to mask any masc features. While there are some great techniques that can be used that look great in photos or on stage, up close they look more like a Lion King the musical face chart. Instead, I'm a big fan of having a painting party and switching off with friends on each other's faces. I was lucky enough to have Miss Fame, Mathu Andersen, and Trixie Mattel paint me for some pics in this book, and I learned a lot each time. One thing we all agree on is the first step to any queen's face should be some good blow. You're gonna wanna blow your nose real well because you can't touch it once you start making up your mug. Snot is a gigantic variable and if you have to blow your nose, there goes the whole bull's-eye of your face.

This is my personal step-by-step to get into full **geish** which you can adapt and use as you please for your own showgirl, date night, or prom mode. You can alternate your base and eye to your liking, but the last few steps should be followed unless you're angling for a mishap. For instance, I like to tuck before I wig up in case my dick-tape gets caught in my hair. Nails should always go on last because if you have to buckle a shoe or give your hose one last tug up, you don't wanna pop a press-on. I tend to give ninety minutes for a full transformation to walk-out-the-door ready. With the right hairstyle, I can cut that down to as little as thirty minutes, depending on the size of the purse I've selected to store the fucks I may or may not chose to give for the evening.

> **❝It is a known fact that a woman *do* carry an evening bag at dinnertime. No lady is sure at night.❞**
>
> **—JUNIOR LABEIJA**

So let's start. This is what I look like without retouching. I'm not trying to live a lie like Kevyn Aucoin's *Making [Photoshop] Faces* book. You know I'm a dude. Plus, Photoshop woulda cost more and and I blew most of the money on strippers and wigs.

I love makeup so much. My mom never wore any makeup, and so I learned about makeup from my dad—specifically, his porn. The '90s was a great time to be a whore, and I loved the smoky eyes that almost every *Playboy* centerfold was sporting.

I start around my eyes because I like to get a really saturated color and not worry about fallout makeup ruining foundation. I pack a ton on and swoop it out with a makeup wipe. You can also use tape or a business card to get a precise line. If one eye is bolder than the other, it's fine. No one's gonna not fuck you 'cause your makeup is uneven. Don't worry. That's what doggy style is for.

1.

1 Rub that eye boogie into your eyelid skin and then take a color similar to whatever the discharge was and highlight your brow bones and inner tear ducts.

2 Line the top lids of your eyes with a pencil, Sharpie or brush dipped in eyeshadow and spit.

3 Shut your eye and go over the lash lines with a brush dipped in dark shadow (brown, navy, or charcoal), hitting your upper and lower lids. Following the orbital

2. *3.* *4.*

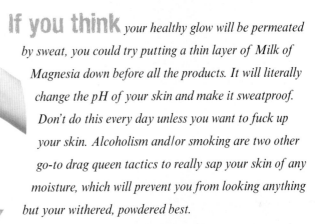

5.

If you think *your healthy glow will be permeated by sweat, you could try putting a thin layer of Milk of Magnesia down before all the products. It will literally change the pH of your skin and make it sweatproof. Don't do this every day unless you want to fuck up your skin. Alcoholism and/or smoking are two other go-to drag queen tactics to really sap your skin of any moisture, which will prevent you from looking anything but your withered, powdered best.*

bones around with the same color works for me. Denying your heritage and just plopping a crease wherever you want on your lids is also an option if you're eyelids are mini garage doors of creaseless flesh.

4 This is the point when you correct any dark circles and beards. Warming up the area with an orangey tone works for me because I'm blond. Darker beards should go with a darker color. I also warm up my crease with some of the same color just 'cause I figured I should look like I tried.

5 Apply a foundation or concealer one shade lighter than the skin under

your eyes, onto the apples of your cheeks, onto the ball and bridge of your nose, and up into the central forehead, and put a dash on the chin. Use a thicker product if you need the coverage due to the fact that you're rotted. Take better care of your skin and maybe get a facial that doesn't come out of a bologna pump once in a while?

6 Apply a foundation or concealer that matches your neck all over everywhere else. You should also decide what you're wearing at this point because it will determine how far down you need this makeup to go. Some queens do Britney, and their nude

illusion is basically a dude's delusion. Their tights are one color, their midriff and arms another color, their neck and titty area yet another shade, and then their mug. Raven is consistently one color and should be everyone's barometer for correctness. I hear she dyes her tights to match. Excuses are useless. Suck less.

6.

7 Now, I'm a very lucky individual. I have more structure in my cheekbones than many have in their entire lives. But contouring can take a girl from a closet-organizing personal shopper who gets pissed on by Brandy's little brother into, well…someone with really good contouring who just stole all of makeup master Scott Barnes's tricks. Scott's skills established JLo's sparkling signature look, and his shading and highlighting techniques have influenced beauty ideals to where they currently sit. He told me to place my contour color under my cheekbones and along the sides of my nose, my chin, and the perimeter of my forehead. This is the third color in the beige rainbow, from the highlight color through multiple foundation tones up to the contour color. You can also add yet another color with some colored hair spray if

7.

you're trying to blend a mannish hairline into a **snatched**-back **bewigglement** on your head. If you're a first-time-in-drag-at-a-ball-er, use evening time tones with evening shade. Don't be a **daywalker**, trying to walk in the day with your newbie contour. Light don't lie and it will expose the structure under the paint you tried to contour. Think of contour as the paint version of when an MTF just pumps her face full of fillers

8.

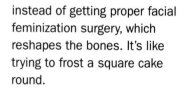

instead of getting proper facial feminization surgery, which reshapes the bones. It's like trying to frost a square cake round.

8 Paint with all the colors of the wind but only if the wind matches your skin tone.

Now, I know this is a *lot*. So let's just put some more shit on shit.

9 At this point, I apply a light mist of an aerosol foundation and use a puff to blend all the edges and set things. Scream a bit and move your face too so you don't have those crevices at the corners of your mouth, nostrils, and eyes that may not be reachable without adjusting your stone-cold **RBF**.

10 Time to cook! Cooking is putting powders in complementary colors over where you just put the creams. I use a fair-colored loose powder in all the highlight spots. Don't use HD (high-

9.

10.

11.

definition) powder. It shows up as white under a flash.

11 Put a powder similar in tone to your contour color in the coordinating areas to cement that color in place. Buff it out a little or don't. You're gonna be dusty as fuck at this point. You may have to face the fug and just give up. It's OK if you feel this way. There's always long bangs, heavy powder, head down, walk fast, no spook (see page 215).

12 If you haven't yet given up, your reward

12.

is glitter. I use it to hide my brows a bit and blur any area where my lack of skill and finesse would otherwise be apparent. I put glitter or just a star sticker on pimples all the time. I'd rather have someone say "You have a piece of

Be careful *taking glitter off. I got a particularly large fleck in my eye as a teen, slept with it in, and woke up with a bloody, crusted pupil. My parents ended up taking me to LensCrafters to get it out, and I ended up telling everyone they took me to the doctor to get the gay outta me, which led to a rumor I was getting gay-conversion therapy. Use painters' tape (or the tape you just peeled off your dick) to get most of it off. If you attempt to wash it off without first trying to remove it dry, as soon as water hits it, the glitter will spread everywhere, and no matter how much you wash, you'll look like one of those Twilight fags in the sun for a day or two.*

something shiny on your face" than "Wow, that looks ready to pop." It's really a Choose Your Own Adventure product. I combine different-size glitters (inset) and then just tap the mixture on.

13 Put a lick of eyeliner on. If you've noticed, we've returned to your eyes. Had we finished them altogether in the first steps, the glitter, liquid eyeliner, and lashes would've gone to shit with all the sprays and powders that have been flying around. Lashes should be devastating, not dustpans.

14 Draw your brows on. If you're a girl and your eyebrows are already where they're supposed to be to make you pretty, well, fine. Why

13.

don't you spend the time you saved by figuring out how not to bleed from your genitals each month? *You're not better than me!*

15 Dust off your extra powders. This is a great time to text your friends that you're running late. When you keep people waiting, that

basically relays that your time is somehow more important than theirs. I have a Rolex, so my time is actually even more valuable, but still—don't be a dickhead.

16 Curl your lashes and put on mascara. Put the wand into the base of your lashes and slowly rotate the

14.

15.

16.

Now, my brows are light because *Jesus loves me and made me blond. If you have to glue them down, do your thing, but do thin layers of glue, letting each dry thoroughly, or it will look like you used Ore-Ida instant mashed potatoes. I also used to sweat a bunch before the*

Botox, and that never helped. So, in keeping with the "Work smarter, not harder" Suck Less mantra, here are some ways to be lazy but look good:

a) **Bleach your brows.** *It changes the whole dynamic of a face. It instantly makes your eyes the darkest thing on your face and thereby the focus, adding smolderocity like you're being lit for a 1940s movie. Once lightened, you can cover them with creams, powders, and a multitude of other shit to hide the actual hair texture. Glue a whole buncha shit to them. Make a butterfly, a gemstone fantasy, or a greasy, mascara-smeared mess.*

For this, I tipped my makeup kit upside down, and any crystals, glitter, or sequins that fell out got glued to my face in Iceland.

b) **Pull your brows up into a more feminine spot by using face tapes.** *This is also great for anyone older, along with distance, darkness, and rose-colored lightbulbs. Miss Fame does this with her face; otherwise, she looks like a transvestite Mr. Magoo.*

c) *Put* **physical barriers** *between other people's eyes and your actual brows: headbands, glasses, fringe/bangs, hats.*

The Rolls Royce of Drag . . .

d) *If you have to* **glue your brows down,** *practice on your hairy-dude feet with the glue or your pubes.*

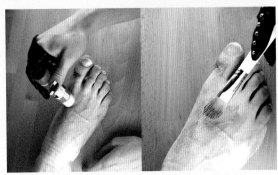

. . . and the Jeep Wrangler of Drag.

HOW TO FAKE A BLACK EYE

*T*he *trashiest sound in America is a woman clicking her tongue ring on her teeth in Walmart. This look evokes all the hallmarks that go along with that mental image. Applying a sallow, yellowish base tone in the orbital perimeter will give dimension to*

bruised tones, which will give the effect you need. Nothing says "I've recently had problems interacting with others" more than facial wounds. People will not *fuck with you when you show up bruised at work. If you're in retail, they'll probably let you just fold shirts in the back instead of dealing with impressionable customers.*

If you're trying to fake it for family court or something, you want to juxtapose it with upstanding things like clean shoes. You can be a wreck from the neck up, but don't be beat up from the feet up. Don't wear sneakers to court ever. PS: If you receive a summons, borrow a baby. Even better if it's a crier. The judge will usually bump up your case to the top of his docket to get rid of the potential disruptions. Babies definitely help with the sympathy factor. I fuck a lawyer and he told me so yeah.

17.

more oomph and trim them so they fit from the center of your pupil to wherever you want them to end. Hit them with a little more mascara because the eyes are the windows to the soul, and my soul is black as fuck.

19 This last pair of lashes can be either the bit you trimmed from the second pair or a new pair. Gluing a section of a spiky or longer lash from the outer pupil to the crease area will help swoop up the whole eye. There is no need to glue the lash to the actual lash line at this point. Nothing wrong with taking a selfie now with your eyes looking down, up, or sideways to plan how to look cute with that night's face.

wand as you pull it out. Like how you would slowly withdraw your dick if the condom broke.

17 Grab a wispy set of lashes that will blend with your own. Test out a strip of lashes and make sure they don't hit the inner brow bone before you've glued them on. Nothing says "I'm an amateur" more than ill-fitting lashes. Trim as needed and glue the sucker to your face. I use tweezers to carefully press them into the still-impressionable mascara. I lightly coat them with more mascara.

18 Take a second pair of lashes with a little

20 Fuck. I forgot to tell you to wash your

18.   *19.*

WILLAM

21.

hands before you started. Sorry.

21 Put a thin coat of mascara on the bottom lashes using the rotating wand trick you probably failed at before. Open your mouth really wide too, because that'll help make you look less stupid, I bet. Now, using tweezers, slide the fake lashes up under the lower lashes and place them next to the actual lashes so they look like they're growing outta your face.

22 Pucker your lips and smile or make whatever stupid face you need to so you can figure out where to put on some blush. You want something glowy that radiates like an Amber Alert. Then put more on, because sometimes it's the only indicator that you're not a dyke.

23 ~~Line~~ Overline your lips with a pencil that's a shade darker than your butthole. Then fill in the entire lip area with a shade matching your asslips. Just peek at your pucker and then you have an honest-to-God nude shade that is perfectly dialed in to your exact complexion. #colormatchyourbutthole.

24 Smear some more shit on your lips. You're probably missing the open bar somewhere and your friends hate you. I personally usually go for the kinda colors I see in the pubic bushes of douche bags who would call me a fag before they got schwasted but will shrug and say YOLO after last call when I'm the last option upright.

25 Do your hair or pick it up off the closet floor. Hopefully, people will like you for your personality. You tried.

22.

23.

24.

25.

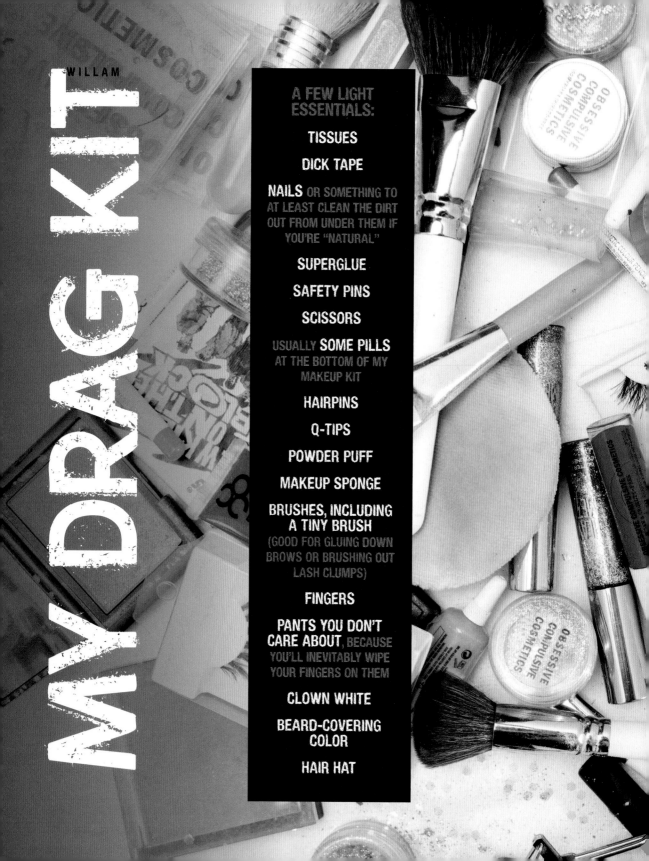

WILLAM

MY DRAG KIT

A FEW LIGHT ESSENTIALS:

TISSUES

DICK TAPE

NAILS OR SOMETHING TO AT LEAST CLEAN THE DIRT OUT FROM UNDER THEM IF YOU'RE "NATURAL"

SUPERGLUE

SAFETY PINS

SCISSORS

USUALLY **SOME PILLS** AT THE BOTTOM OF MY MAKEUP KIT

HAIRPINS

Q-TIPS

POWDER PUFF

MAKEUP SPONGE

BRUSHES, INCLUDING A TINY BRUSH (GOOD FOR GLUING DOWN BROWS OR BRUSHING OUT LASH CLUMPS)

FINGERS

PANTS YOU DON'T CARE ABOUT, BECAUSE YOU'LL INEVITABLY WIPE YOUR FINGERS ON THEM

CLOWN WHITE

BEARD-COVERING COLOR

HAIR HAT

**THREE SHADES OF
HEAVY CONCEALER
OR BASE** (ONE IN YOUR
SKIN TONE, ONE A SHADE
LIGHTER, AND ONE A SHADE
DARKER)

CONTOUR SHADE
(CREAM AND POWDER)

FOUNDATION
(AEROSOL OR LIQUID)

HIGHLIGHT POWDER
(FAIR, BUFF, OR BANANA)

BLUSH

GLITTER
(CREAM AND LOOSE)

EYELASH CURLER
(I USE THE BILLY B ONE
SINCE HE TOLD ME IT'S
BETTER COPY OF THE
KEVYN AUCOIN ONE, WHICH
WAS A COPY OF THE SHU
UEMURA)

LASHES (I HAVE THREE
PAIRS ON THE TOP AND ONE
ON THE BOTTOM)

ELMER'S GLUE
(PURPLE ONE)

BLACK EYELINER

LIQUID EYELINER

MASCARA

EYE SHADOW

BROW COLOR

LIP PENCILS

LIP COLOR

How to **SUCK LESS** at

BEING A HAIRLESS CREATURE OF GOD

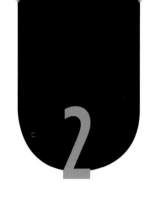

I am not a Kardashian fan. That being said, I'm also not an anti-Kardashian. They're smart, or, if not, at least smart enough to get smarter people than them to handle their empires. They let others tend to their business and branding opportunities in the fields of sex tapes, hair extensions, and affordable fashions by Kmart because they're busy taking selfies and getting hair removal probably. Armenians are hairy as fuck, and that's coming from an Italian cross-dresser. The Kardashian women have been up front about the massive amounts of hair removal they've undergone, and I respect the fuck outta them for that. I've electrolyzed my chest, lasered my balls and no!no!'d my no-no parts. I appreciate each Kim, Kourt, and Khatever because it looks like they probably waxed everything from their bottom lash down. Which is a good thing, because an Armenian wiping their ass can be like getting peanut butter out of a shag carpet.

Now, here's the thing about hair down there: Say I invite someone over for sex and explain, "Hey, I have a dog." It's a fair warning there might be a chew toy or maybe a pee-pee pad. But if I open the door and it looks like I actually have an ape with an attitude problem, it's not justified. Like, it's cool to have a dog, and everyone knows dogs can be a mess, just like everyone knows hair grows down there. It's up to you to keep it in check.

What I'm saying is to at least trim that shit. Like, give it a blunt edge. You don't want it long enough that you can identify a curl pattern or dye swatch. Like "Oh, your chest hair is a 27 honey blond with a loose body wave." I want as little variation as possible in that below-the-equator area. Is almost cutting piss parts in the shower fun for anyone? No. Razors, plucking, and waxing are taxing. I prefer for my Hot Pocket not to look like its microwave-safe cooking sleeve is actually a bath mat made of pubes. But again—you do you regarding your crotch and all. But just so you know, socially acceptable pubes usually range somewhere between "some" and "enough to exfoliate your partner's face off."

LASER works the same as tattoo removal. It focuses on the color in the hair follicle and zaps it to the root the same way tattoo removal technology works (i.e., yellow, white, and light inks are virtually impossible to remove). Pain-wise, it's basically like snapping a rubber band on your skin. A lot. Not enough to throb afterward but enough to annoy you and make you wanna smack a bitch. It works best on dark hair with light skin. Blond hair and red hair on tan skin are the hardest, hence I've relied on…

ELECTROLYSIS uses direct current via an electrode needle, set off while inserted next to the hair shaft just under your skin. This has the best and most proven results, but it's also the most painful. I had ingrowns galore throughout the year I did this because it basically kills the hair in the follicle, and that dies and falls out. The bulb then rests for a minute and grows a new hair, which sometimes has trouble breaking through the skin and curls up inside itself (that's an ingrown). This cycle of grow and zap usually takes two or more tries before that hair will not be seen again. Keep in mind, some follicles have two or three hairs growing out of them, so the procedure will sound like a bug zapper sometimes. Seriously, look down your shirt at your nipple. Now, really look at your nipple like the dirty little chew toy it is. You'll see some of the hair follicles around it have multiple hairs growing from them. Betcha didn't know that, huh? The pain level on electrolysis was enough to make me smoke some weed before I went in each time. With laser and electrolysis, you can say **BGB** to the tough choice of whether it's cool to use the same razor for your asshole and face. It was always such a moral dilemma for me.

Say *no* to any As Seen on TV shit like that zappity-zap piece of shit that advertises heavenly pulses of pain-free light to get rid of hair. That boat don't float.

SHAVING is a great, but don't be fooled by multiple-blade gimmickry. Sometimes one blade is the best way to avoid ingrowns and bumps. Lemme splain. See, the first blade that catches the hair pulls it and stretches it, then the following blade(s) snaps it off, making it want to curl and retract up under the skin, like what a rubber band does when it breaks. That can cause an ingrown. Better to single-blade it or take your time with a multiblade. Always shave in the direction the hair grows in areas where friction can occur, like your thigh gap or any chub-rub areas you might have. Take care not to shave areas that rub together before activities because your own thighs can create a ham sandwich of heated friction that isn't on anyone's menu.

DEPILATORIES like Nair are great but can irritate the skin. You also can't do anything else really while using them if you don't want to fuck up your furniture, answer your door, or scare the fuck outta anyone you're staying with.

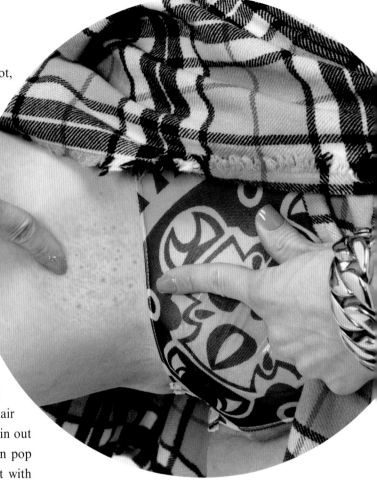

WAXING rips the hair out by the root, and the results last at least twice as long as shaving. Don't do this and hit the beach; I did it, and two days later I had a bump garden no one wanted to visit. It was either one of two things or a mix of the two: folliculitis, which is an irritation of the skin resulting in whiteheads—the worst chub rub ever—or ingrown hairs. Ingrown hairs can be cured only by removal or the little fuckers growing out on their own (don't hold your breath). The worst part about waxing is allowing the hair to get long enough for you to actually go through with it.

Soaking a cloth in hot Epsom-salted water and applying it to the ingrown hair area really helps alleviate it. It dries the skin out and eliminates bacteria so new growth can pop through undeterred. Picking the hairs out with dirty safety pins is my favorite way but not recommended unless you're a skank. Both folliculitis and ingrowns are best treated with exfoliation and Tend Skin (an over-the-counter beta hydroxy, which means it's a light acid that will burn the shit outta your skin, removing the top layer, thereby giving the impacted hairs a better chance of poking through). It's a godsend for making sure your beard doesn't look all Nestlé Crunch textured

At least nothing is seeping, right?

after shaving too frequently or too close, or from using that slightly rusted razor on the edge of the tub from last week. The level of sting when applying a beta hydroxy is like if you're eating salt-and-vinegar chips while you have a cold sore, but it's totally worth the purchase.

How to **SUCK LESS** at
COVERING SKIN PROBLEMS

Skin issues are a surefire way to make you not wanna go outside. It's, like, the worst thing ever. What's the second worst thing? Clowns. So if you combine them, the double negative equals a positive.

Everyone from Boy George and Leigh Bowery to Rihanna has used tranimalistic (punk + clown + avant-garde = tranimal) methods to achieve fierce looks. Try placing a fishnet stocking or anything with a texture on your face after your foundation and apply color to achieve a pattern that will maybe mask the irregularity of cystic acne.

Shoot for the stars, 'cause you'll never be one. The iconic Raven told Tyra that and, oooops, she wasn't wrong. Some reality shows purport to find the next big something but fail more often than they succeed. #FACT. So if you want a constellation worth of stars, just use the backing of a sheet of some star stickers, apply makeup like a stencil, and serve straight-up planetarium puss.

Or just go straight-up whore clown and cover what you need to cover with clown white and glitter.

Page 20's look is just about flawless skin. Some would say it's a plain or neutral face, but I think highlighting the natural beauty of the skin is all you really need when you have a giant herpes sore pulsating along to the very beat of its host's heart. I've been getting cold sores in the same spot on my lip since I was a kid, and I know plenty of other people who have been getting them waaaay before they coulda gotten herpes from doing anything fun and sticky. I have no shame in talking about it. I had a first-grade photo of me with a scabby lip, and I was called Herpules by my classmates every time I had one. I only ever got them from stress. So of course when writing this book I thought, "I should really talk about covering scabs or cold sores 'cause plenty of people get them," but then I crossed it out because no one on Craigslist replied to my ad seeking their scabby services. But lo and behold, when the writing was complete and I started shooting the pics for *Suck Less*, I got one.

I prefer an aerosol foundation (like Diorskin Airflash) when I have a cold sore, because semi-seeping scabs are like good English muffins: They got hella nooks and crannies, and you wanna get full coverage without disrupting the healing process by touching them a bunch. Don't

use a brush, because you'll run the risk of forgetting to wash it and then use it again. Eww. Random bit of Willam wisdom: If you're prone to
cold sores, try to eat foods high in lysine (seafood,
eggs, beans, meat, and cheese) and avoid putting
into your body foods with lots of acidity or argi-
nine and especially genitalia with scabbing.

ABOVE: Wig: James the Gemini. Cold Sore: Model's own.
RIGHT: This makeup was a Herpulean effort.

How to **SUCK LESS** at
ZITS

You ever pop a zit so big you swear it squeals like a lobster hitting hot water? I know it's fun and it makes you feel like you actually are taking control of the situation, but in reality, you're making it worse. Whiteheads happen when oil is trapped in a pore on your face. The best general way to remove these if you have a ton of them is with what can be considered an over-the-counter peel with some ingredients in it that are hard to pronounce (I like Neutrogena Healthy Skin Face Lotion with alpha hydroxy). If you just try to pop them, chances are you'll force the pore clog down further into your skin and you'll increase the chances of residual redness, inflammation, and your genitals not being caressed by others.

Blackheads are simply whiteheads that have oxidized, meaning the clog has been open to the air and turns a darker color. If you squeeze your nose and pus comes out, you should maybe not do that 'cause it's nasty. If you do it anyway, the best spot to wipe your hand is the back lower leg of your pants. No one notices stains there.

Now, figure out why these blemishes are present. Is your hair greasy? Do you wash your makeup off but forget to wash your ears? Do you get beard burn on your face when you make out with dudes with goatees? I never understand people who can fall asleep in their drag or makeup. The best part about getting it all off you is blowing your nose in the shower. You feel so much better after clearing the pipes.

I know no one wants bad skin, but just going at your face with whatever you think will help is about as useful as doing your hair with a dick. My skin problems were caused by a multitude of factors. I was using too much of the wrong makeup. I mistakenly assumed that since Proactiv was good enough for Jessica Simpson, it was good enough for me. In addition, I was on planes almost every other day, which made my skin dryer than Waffle House hash browns and just as scattered, smoth-

If you find *yourself taking off your makeup in a remote location, you can make your own wet wipes by just blowing your nose. It's your own snot so you can't get an infection from it (I think), and it totally gets off eye makeup.*

ACCUTANE is a miracle drug for acne. But if you're a girl and you get pregnant on it, you'll need an actual miracle worker like Helen Keller. Your baby will be retarded and deaf and probably not so hot as a contributing member of society. There is a 100 percent chance of some sort of birth defect. So every pill you take has a pregnant-lady peel-back tab with a big red warning on it to not get knocked up. I can only have butt babies, so I made cute nails out of them. The other side effects include mood swings, dry eyes, additional mood swings (since you can't drink on it), nosebleeds, and my cracked, chapped lips. On the upside, I had *zero* blackheads. For someone who's tried everything, even putting my own piss on my face like a toner, it was a godsend.

ered and bothered. Stress was also a major issue. (I was regularly performing in a trio called DWV, and issues with the D and V members of the group forced me to downsize into just meWme. I'd say D and V were the cause of my stress, but I should note that comparing my former coworkers to actual VD is unfair to venereal diseases.) My face got better once I eliminated the stressors and started on a skin regime of simple Neutrogena products and a round of Accutane (Roaccutane in Australia).

Since you were nice enough to buy my book, I will give you a foolproof pimple technique.

Now that I've told you these things, here's the part where you ignore all of it and have a pick party. Clean a needle with fire, alcohol, or spit, depending on your desired level of sterility, and then lance the nastiness straight through the top of the peak. Use cotton swabs on each side to squeeze it until what comes out looks like the watery red pre-cum stuff a ketchup bottle releases before the actual ketchup. Let it sit for a second, and clear the area. Then go in for the last squeeze to get the core out. Now wipe the mirror, pig.

1.   *2.*

1 Get an Advil Liqui-Gel and pierce it with a pin.

2 Squeeze some of the gel onto the pimple and the pimple kinda magically disappears in a few hours. I don't know why this works. I'm not a scientist. But it does. And if it doesn't work on you or gives you some kinda chemical burn, fuck off completely. I'm a drag queen.

SOME MORE HOW-TO TIPS:

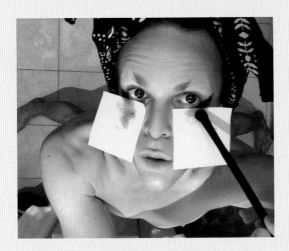

1 Avoid eye makeup fallout if you do foundation before eye makeup with Post-it's!

2 Making marbleized lips (as on the title page) is easy. Dip little pieces of card stock into swirled liquid lipstick (preferably OCC); then stamp it onto your lips.

3 There's an art to humblebrag pics. Clearly, I'm showing off my shitter in the example, but my caption would read something like "#CLAWPOWER" and thanking the manicurist. You're never too old for that whorey look.

4 Shove a safety pin or hairpin through the end of your spliff or blunt to stay burn-free when there's not enough finger space.

How to **SUCK LESS** at
LEAVING THE HOUSE

My grandma Belli was a good Italian wife who got a scholarship to Juilliard for music, raised five kids, and bowled a 260. She also lived in sunny Florida and had stage 4 melanoma for eight years of her life. I got a buncha good *Golden Girls* wicker purses when she passed, though, so it's not a totally bad story. The point is, tanning is bad. Sure, I've said stuff in the past, like "Tan fat is better than pale fat." I totally stand by that, and if you're fat, you should, too. Literally. Stand your fat ass up, 'cause the traditional lie-down tanning bed will leave you with streaks on your sides if you're big. Plus, you can do squats in there and it's like Bikram without all the yoga twats. There are plenty of good self-tanners out there. Fuck cancer.

I always have a garbage bag with me in case someone I meet is ugly. It's also good for when the weather is iffy and you don't wanna tote around an umbrella. Not a giant Hefty one or nothing. Just a thin one that you can poke a head hole in and wear as a poncho in a pinch. Also great for outdoor concerts and festivals that get moist. No one wants to get hit by your soggy umbrella at the concert when whoever's onstage says, "Put your hands up!" Oh yeah... That's the other thing. If you're at a concert and somebody with a mic yells "Where all my ladies at?" I'm gonna be the loudest "*Haaaa-eeeey*." It'll be like a three-syllable "Hey." Don't be embarrassed. I just want everyone around me to know that the gay contingent is in the vicinity and present. We are gonna be loud and have fun and dance 'cause it's a concert. If you ain't into it, best to maybe try a dinner theater and sit the fuck down. I fag out hard and I fag out early. I will tell it on a mountain and yell "Yes, bitch!" at any little riff of a run. I'll "Mmmmmphm" real loud at a good part, like I just had the best bite of ribs ever, and I'll do it harder if I catch any side eye from anybody.

Speaking of ribs, don't ever go out without eating beforehand. You ever get in a line for a club or concert and some bitch behind you has takeout, and you're like "Damn, I'm in my cute going-out clothes and now it smells like onions"? The upside is now you won't feel bad about letting your friend cut the line to stand by you. So no eating in line, and don't try to be a buddy to my bully and offer me some grub. It may be cute for you to try to cover up chicken taco burps with some Trident, but I'm here to get fucked up and not worry about taking a deuce at this spot.

"I like tans on my legs but not on my face. *Shut up!*" Trust me. Google that quote and have a say-something hat day.

How to **SUCK LESS** at

TATTOOS

HERE ARE SOME GUIDELINES SO YOUR INK DON'T STINK.

1 Have your tattoo be of some use to you or others. Maybe an important reminder to just be the yin to nature's yang and breathe. Just kidding. Your body is gonna breathe whether you want it to or not. And the only thing worse than a yin-yang tattoo is a No Fear T-shirt slogan or a Chinese symbol that probably has meant something different to every Panda Express employee who's laughed at you. My tattoo is useful because I'm basically the Swiss Army knife of transvestites. I always got a ruler on me no matter what. My dad asked me what happens if I move to Europe with the metric system, and I assuaged his fears by telling him that all the good stuff is still measured in inches there (dicks and hair weave lengths).

2 Think of it as permanent jewelry, like my friend Kain.

3 Coulda left off the "ogies" but to each their own.

4 Never put a name near a sex organ. Too many questions. My name is inches from this lady's butthole, for some reason. It's almost as bad as a tramp stamp that says "She get it from her daddy."

5 Nothing trendy. Bands break up and teams get traded all the time. Sorry. RIP DWV.

6 Be ready for ignorance. Some older folks think visible tats are the death of any employment future, so that kind of prejudice is something you need to be ready to encounter. For instance, some asshole once said, "You wanna fuck a guy with a neck tattoo, not date a guy with one," and that's

mostly true (I was the asshole). It's mostly because neck tattoos are basically Viagra for anyone with a penchant for getting banged out by bad boys, so there's not a chance a neck-tatted man can be faithful with all the ass being thrown at him. It's like FaceTiming the pope to say grace. Or trying to have stained glass etched on your body and ending up with plain ass. My face in this tattoo needs the lord also.

(7) Don't get a tattoo that you have to shave for it to look good. I had enough beard issues that I don't need your forearm fur adding more shade.

5-7 inches: Dollar Dicks are penises that are about 6in/15cm on average. These are penises that you may not necessarily have to do a full on douche before bologna-ponying if you do a thorough enough shower. But remember if it starts to smell or feel like you're roasting a turdle dove, don't try to fuck your way through it and think "I can get him off before it gets really bad." All the fucking & motion will create radiant energy and greenhouse effect the room further concentrating that shitshock smell.

7-9 inches: Dongs have a certain amount of heft. Think how a regular clock ticks or beeps but a grandfather clock goes "dong." Like that. Many of the people who possess appendages in this range know they have a healthy slab on them. For instance, it's definitely a Dong if the owner says something rhetorical like "Tell me how much you like this Dong" while you're sucking it even though you obviously like it cause it's in your mouth. Duh.

9+ inches: Narnia Cock is big enough to predicate that no food is consumed pre-intercourse due to the fact that Narnia Cock's reach and range will go beyond the normal lower rectum. Narnia Cock is no joke. Remember, Aslan was a noble lion, not a shitty kitty. Come correct.

When I'm stuck with a day that's gray and lonely, I just stick my fist in my mouth and make hot guys with tattoos touch me for money—which also brings to mind my favorite way to catch a hooker who's not using his own pictures. Keep the ad up when they walk into a room so if their tatts or general appearance don't match their pic, you can handle it. Buyer beware. Speaking of, if you're planning on major ink, have the money allocated for it before you start. I know this one hooker named Brandon who I wanted to do a GoFundMe for his incomplete full back piece but hey outta sight, outta mind.

31

HOW TO **SUCK LESS** AT
PIERCINGS

A genital piercing is like fighting. It always sounds like a great idea at first, but you might fuck up your teeth. I had to spend almost $1,200 to fix my veneers even though the material is supposed to be stronger than a toilet bowl. I had my guiche/taint pierced, and one guy literally looked at it and said, "I'm not into that," and left. I woulda been sad, but this is why you always have a backup butt buddy. I liked my taint barbell because it felt good every time I sat down. It was perfectly lined up with my prostate (that little spot you can press behind your balls that feels good). But if you get pierced in the wrong spot, it's like putting a door knocker on a screen door—totally useless. With the right spot, you can sit on a hard surface and just gently rock back and forth, playing with that spot without even a hand check. It's like edging for your butthole. Sluts know what I mean. Some shops won't do any sort of genital piercings. It's a very personal area, so you can't, like, just faggily run up into Claire's, trying to get your nipple pierced and screaming about discrimination upon denial.

I pierced my own nipple to get sent home from school in ninth grade. There was a test and I wanted out, so me and a safety pin went to town. It worked. The second time I pierced that nipple was when I was playing Joseph in *Joseph and the Amazing Technicolor Dreamcoat*. It may not have been historically accurate, but it distracted from the fact that I had on more makeup than all the Rockettes put together. The third time I pierced both and that was the last. I ended up taking them out when I got liposuction and not putting them back in. If I squeeze my nipples now, a little drop of yellow smegma-looking stuff comes out to this day, reminding me of my poor judgment.

I subscribe to the school of thought that when pissing, I don't have to wash my hands if I don't touch my dick (pull down flop out and use elbow/foot to flush). If you have a Prince Albert, you will have to plug the second hole if you take it out or risk a secondary stream of pee.

Labia, hood, and clit piercings are all fine, but just know that gravity is a sin and those little piercings are like vagina weights and can turn your lady bits into some Laffy Taffy stretched-out shit. Don't do too large a jewelry gauge down there.

Let this serve as a warning that some holes never close and refined sugar is the devil.

What's the quickest way for a white girl to get keloids? Supergluing earrings to your lobes. Put medical tape or Band-Aids down first and then the glue if regular earring backs aren't enough. Or be that rotted queen deformed by drag. Your call.

How to **SUCK LESS** at

HAIR

I came out as a lifestyle guru at eight years old, when I marched into my mother's room and said, "Hey, guess what? I can French braid!" Without even looking up, she said, "Oh good. Just what every mother wants to hear from her firstborn son."

I bought my first wig at a thrift store and tried desperately to make her blond. I brought the good Garnier Nutrisse box dye because SJP was in the commercials and I loved her. When it didn't work, I used peroxide. Then bleach. #FAIL. I realized that it wasn't dyeable because it was a synthetic fiber. Later in life, I learned that the only way to transform a synthetic wig into human hair is to have a man ejaculate in it and clap real loud at the same time.

Hair coloring was always so fascinating to me because it could make or break a career. Norma Jean Blahnd vs. Platinum Marilyn. Gays and girls alike have had obsessions with single-process divas for years. Cher is black as a motherfuck. Reba is a brick of red with not a lowlight. Remember mousy-brown Christina post-mouseketeering that *Mulan* song? You could tell she hated singing about her boring reflection so fuckin' much, and that's probably why she took to the Clorox.

There's something about all that artificiality that makes a person gravitate toward it. Anyone who's ever bleached their hair knows what it's like to pick those fun little scabs in the back by the neck two days after processing. Then you're all like "OMG, I have those scabs too!" It's sad for them but makes me appreciate their efforts. I'm pulling for them. Just like each New Year's Eve, I make a resolution for this to be the year Rachel McAdams finally gets her hair game together. I mean, girl… *True Detective*? Sure, solve crimes and shit, but ol' Lady *Murder, She Wrote* Lansbury had time for a rinse-and-roller set, and so do you. Lady cop all you want, but you cannot be cavalier about touch-ups on those roots and expect a consistent color. Hair color has chemicals that work in conjunction with the heat coming off your scalp, so if there's too much regrowth, the color doesn't process. Especially if you're using bleach. Golden halos are like piss rings of yellow around your head and occur when the new blond doesn't match the previous blond. Roots are OK in your hair or wig— *if* it's styled. Without the finesse of a "done" style, you risk looking like the eighth mug shot in a series of ten pics showing a meth user from ages twenty-eight to forty-two. You want that hair to look *paid* and *laid*, honey. Even ombré has its limits.

We should probably talk about wigs now too, 'cause when someone asks "Is that your hair?" they probably already know it isn't. I do it all the time just so I don't feel as bad about the mess going on with my scalp. So don't bother lying. It's fine to throw in some fake hair, extensions, pieces, or whatev.* But treat it like a top-secret crime and cover your tracks—especially if you're a man. This man-bun trend doesn't seem to be bottoming out anytime soon, but bottoming out is the only thing you'll be doing if you're a man with visibly fake hair. Call me old-fashioned, but you cannot reasonably ask to top a man while wearing someone else's hair. Above all, your man hair should look like you didn't spend a lot of time on it if you want it to appear effortless. Think archetypes of manhood: Steve McQueen, Idris Elba, Patrick Swayze, Jason Momoa. Even if they did spend time getting perms, edge-ups, and color, it didn't look it.

It's smart to factor in the amount of upkeep that will be necessary should you decide that the hair on your head will not be the stuff that's grown from your scalp. Don't do any drastic hair changes if your money situation isn't solid. You never want to have to choose between gas money or getting your extensions out. If whoever is grabbing your ass that month thinks you look good blond, ask for money when it comes time to get your hair done. Where I grew up in Philly, most of the women got their men to pay for their hair appointments, which is weird because the men probably never got to touch it after it was installed.

Speaking of fake hair, test-run a look before making the change with your own locks. Go to a wig store, buy a wig cap for however much they charge, and try some wigs until the Asian lady starts to yell. I have no clue why all hair stores are run by Asian people, yet it's still racist if a white person wants to do braids. I think any hairstyle can be worn by anyone. Like, I'm not going to go into the Chickenhead No Mo salon in Inglewood and say "Gimme the 'Beyoncé Goes to Haiti' braids." That would be culturally insensitive. It's

---

* If we're out and about and you see me, don't yell "I like your wig." "Wig" is such a clinical word, like "homosexual" or "discharge." You can say "Now, that is a nice hat, sirma'am." Or mention how nice my unit is looking despite the club's bad ventilation and humidity. Never touch a drag queen above her chin unless invited. Just a fist bump away. Don't put your arm around her shoulders too much either, because that makes her wig wanna run away from her forehead. Kinda yanks a bitch back along with hair to which the wig is pinned.

called a box braid. Learn your shit. If you're buying a wig and think you're being overcharged, the best thing to do is notate the manufacturer on the tag and maybe the model number on the box. Google will tell you how much it costs online and you can know if you're being ripped off (they will always try to rip you off, especially in October because of Halloween).

Like any structure, a wig needs a good foundation. A wig cap is your best bet if your hair isn't thick enough to hold a hairpin without slippage. Tape or a sticky ACE bandage around the

Make me tan!

perimeter of the head works too if you plan on **shablamgeling** all over the dance floor or speed-boating. I like to bust the wig cap open at the top and pull it down to my neck like a choker. That way, when I pull it up, all the little baby neck hairs and circumferential hairs are slicked up into it and not poking out the sides. Crosshatching the pins at four to six junctures on the head should keep it in place, depending on the style and weight of the unit you're sporting.

I personally like to double my facial width with hair as a minimum (meaning if your face is ten inches across, have at least five inches of hair on each side and five on top). Bigger hair makes a face appear more petite, obviously. If you have the kinda lovely face that can pull off a short hair gig, go for it. But let me tell you a story: When I first started doing shows, I met Morgan McMichaels for the first time, and I learned two things: (1) She does a fierce Annie Lennox, and (2) she must not have had any friends to tell her she needs to paint the back of her neck when she does the bus-driver-lady short wigs. You don't want your face from Brazil and your neck from Scotland. Guys, this goes for you, too. No one wants the back and side of your neck looking like a happy trail. If you ain't found the kinda buddy who will check for errant hairs and shoulder zits, maybe just ask

whoever of your friends is the biggest and most likely hairiest. I had a standing date once a month to buzz my one big friend's back during summer and he sure would smoke me out and let me eat whatever I wanted from his fridge. I know he'd rather just do it himself, but **ABC**.

Chances are a wig straight outta the bag is not gonna be as flattering to your face as it is to the little white Styrofoam head. Make that friend who does hair come over to trim it to fit your features better or hit Fantastic Sams for a bang trim. Take your Friday wig out of the bag on Thursday night and hang it upside down so it'll get some good lift to it. It'll save you some back-combing, but definitely throw in a good base tease. You want it to move when you move. Big hair doesn't have to mean helmet hair. Synthetic hats will keep a style longer than human hair, but they will also tangle much quicker. Throwing a bag of human hair up into a fake can make for a nice blend, which splits the difference: the good structure of an unnatural fiber with the touchability of actual hair at the bottom. When a wig gets too ratty, you can always dread it up or make it into a mufasa. (A mufasa is a wig consisting of many other wig parts and/or tracks that looks like a lion's mane. It's where a weave that might be past its glory days can do a circle of life for all tranimals under the sun.)

DIVA HAIR™

This is my math face.

1.

*Every generation has a diva with an iconic mop that has all the queens scratching their head on how to replicate it. Think of Chaka Khan's Muppet-hooker look. Another would be Madonna's alopecia-inducing braid/**snatched**-back ponytail combo in* Truth or Dare. *The newest entries into who I think will be a fag fan for life is Ms. Ariana Grande. Here's how to do her swingy pony, half up, half down gig but a little draggier. 'Cause no dude looks good in a slick-back on top. You need some volume to even out your big man head probably, and wigs are sized for regular lady heads. Just trust me. So here you go. I present to you the Ariana Grangbang Schtupdo. It's good, sexy hair.*

1 Get a base wig that fits your hairline well along with two ponytails or falls in the same tone. I Sharpied in a bit of a root on mine. The markers that are normally used to touch up woodwork on furniture work good, too. Pin it into toupee clips that you've secured at the temples and on the back of your head. You wanna be able to suck dick in a hurricane in this hair. Make sure you have enough pins crosshatched in a halo around your head.

2 Next, you're gonna wanna use a heat protectant. By that, I mean hit a bowl.

3.

6.

3 Pull the top (and sides, if you want) up into a ponytail and back-comb it until it looks like a shelter dog with mange. You can also ball up another wig and pin it to the top of that wig and use it as a "bump." *Side note: Wigs are a frequent spot to hide drugs during travel, so your bump can actually hold bumps.*

6 Pin the second ponytail under the first to give you some length right through the Wigs By Vanity tag. Yes. I said Wigs By Vanity. That's WigsByVanity.com.

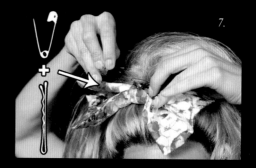

7.

4.

4 Take your first ponytail and pin it into the ratted-up hair underneath it. Be thorough because this is the first thing a bitch will grab if shit gets rowdy. Nothing like grabbing some ho by her ponytail only to swing her around by it to beat her face. I love fighting. It makes me feel alive.

5 Wrap a piece of hair around the base of the ponytail to hide your pin work.

7 You could be done now, but I come from the shit-on-shit school of thought. Nothing says I tried my best to look like a woman like a simple bow. The best method to pin something large into your hair is to stick a sturdy safety pin through the base of whatever it is and then pin the bow into place as desired. This is especially useful for pinning in flowers through the stem.

Look at how classy I look. I could go to fuckin' Easter in that.

How to **SUCK LESS** at

SHOES

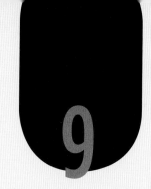

My first pair of heels was given to me by my dad, a former marine. They were a pair of wood clogs with a three-inch block at the back that he wore in the '70s. They click-clacked like my favorite RuPaul song (now available on iTunes). I'm sure he didn't see it as giving me heels, but he was also cool enough not to give a shit when I was sent home from eighth grade for violating the dress code.

My second pair of heels was procured on a shopping trip at fourteen with my aunt Nancy's then-girlfriend, now-wife DJ. Convincing a man

who said "Oo-rah" and a lady who likes hoo-ha's to gimme the shoes was the easy part. The first few times I tried on high heels I probably looked like a crackhead trying to stand up in a canoe. I actually know what that looks like too, because I lived on a creek in South Jersey for a minute, and when my relatives would get outta rehab, they'd usually visit us instead of going straight back to Philly.

Anyway, walking in heels is not all that hard as long as you take it step by step. OMG, I didn't even plan that joke. I was just typing stream of consciousness, wondering WTF I was gonna write, and it happened (Books are hard). I couldn't use my looks, luck, or backup singers when I decided to write it and just had to commit. Kinda like heels. You're gonna have to give up the notion that your feet won't hurt at first. That's why you should try on a lot of heels if you're a first-time shopper. I subscribe to the school of thought that a good heel should be the size of a good dick (when flaccid): nothing under three and a half inches. But if you're just starting or have smaller feet, maybe try a wedge or something lower. I think shoes really say a lot about a

Remember how Michelle Visage called Latrice Royale's boots "lesbian hiking boots"? Well, guess what my first pair of heels was: the same shoe. (Hi, Michelle!)

person. Mine all give the suggestion that, "yes, I will do anal, and how kind of you to notice my hindquarters."

The whole reason I got the idea to write this book is because a friend asked me for drag help. When I couldn't tutor in person, I wrote lady lists and sent Vimeo-protected, password-personalized tuck videos to peruse. But heels we always did in person because it's not the kinda thing you can just take a correspondence course for.

If you're a dude, it's always a smart idea to get a sturdier shoe, because tippy tumbles will happen. Watching Neil find his stride in heels for *Hedwig and the Angry Inch* made me glad the shoes he had were reinforced. That's a great trick, BTW. If you're a newbie, take your heels to a cobbler and they can put in a small brace to make them sturdier. You're most likely gonna be dealing with spilled drinks somewhere, so take all the help you can get. Neil took to it quickly because he's, well, basically good at everything. It's way more fun when people aren't as agile as him. You-Tube 'drag queens falling' and you'll agree. I have a four-inch scar on the inside of my leg from my freshman year homecoming after-party, when I decided I should wear all the high heels and do a one man walk off. Also, men (and girls with big tits) tend to have to deal with looking like a top-heavy gorilla in a race to see how fast they can fall to the floor.

One of the notes I found myself repeating from the NPH movement sessions was to slow down. When you rush, your shoulders rise and you hunch up like a linebacker. I remind myself to keep my shoulders down and my neck long, and it really helps propel the 150 pounds of man more gracefully, even though I'm walking on toothpicks. Your tits will look better, too. Sit into each step, and put your foot down before you pick the other one up. This also helps with not tripping because you have to make contact with your heel first and roll through the front of your foot. If you're a guy and you want to walk in heels, you naturally have it a little harder than a woman because your center of gravity is lower. Women have shorter torsos and lower fulcrums than men. (The fulcrum is the point where your body bends when you fall over 'cause you don't know how not to go ass up and out.)

Know that if you're in a heel, you're bound to garner more attention. No one should be looking at anything else in the room if a bitch is on a runway and has got a good pump in her pumps going. Girls and fags will be checking out your shoe game, and admirers will get a better view of your ass since heels make the peaches more pert. Seeing Raja or Mathu at the top of a runway gets me excited because I know I'm about to see a feat that looks effortless but in actuality combines athleticism while balancing restraint and showmanship. It's all a show—and what do you do before a show? You practice. Any time a normal person sees a dark parking garage, I see a runway. I know some like to cross their left foot in front of their right foot for each step, and there are those who pretend to walk an imaginary tightrope. I prefer to sit into each step and let my hip roll through to the next sauntery step. Your walk will come to you over time. Copying some runway model's stride is never a good idea for starters. For one, you're not a model. Models don't read books and you're, like, forty-something pages up into this bitch.

Paint all the piggies even if only two or three show through any peep toes. What if there's an after-party and you wanna kick off your shoes? Or some hot dude is into feet but your lazy ass didn't wanna spend five more seconds on each foot? Your pinkie toenail is probably the size of a piece of gravel, yet you can't be bothered? *Bye.*

How to **SUCK LESS** at

LOOKING RIGHT

10

Taking a good picture can be easy if you don't overthink it. It's best to blast any thoughts you may have out of your brain with awesome music. You want a good beat and something that makes you wanna bop but not quite boogie, 'cause you need to pose long enough to get the shot. Having a few drinks or whatever is also totally recommendable to loosen you up. Not enough to be messy, although falling in pictures does make for great images. (See below.) I fuckin' ate it, but I got the shot.

If you ever brain-fart out on poses, just pretend to be anyone with a better life. Seeing how awesome Christie Brinkley's life is in "Uptown Girl" makes me happier than videos of deaf babies hearing for the first time. So happy. So does pretending to be Gigi Gorgeous. In my favorite-ever Instagram of Gigi, she was serving it up—literally…cranberry sauce three days after Thanksgiving. I was like "WTF? You're Canadian and your Thanksgiving was in October. Put down the fuckin' gravy boat." But I still favorited it and

retweeted. She's my biggest shim-spiration at the moment.

Now, if you're a guy, you may wanna steer clear of pretending to be a rich white woman. You can still keep holiday-related condiments on hand to overpose with. Making sex-related faces always works well, too. Visualize that moment when the dick feels bigger than it looks, or furrow your brow like somebody's pussy is looser than it should be. Gape the mouth open like you're riding reverse cowgirl with one foot on the dresser. Replicate the agony/ecstatcy face of when your dick is sucked one millisecond too long after cumming. It's like all the despair of a generation combined with wondering if it's too late to get pizza. If you're planning on having a lot of skin out or being full-on naked for your modelings, pull an Amanda Lepore and take off all your clothes immediately once you get to the set (optional: bring a loose robe), so you don't have lines to retouch from waistband indentations, sock marks, etc. You need a good two hours for those to go away once they're there.

All the makeup in the world around those five holes on your face won't help if you don't know what to do with your face. I rely on three looks.

My first agency card. She thought she was sooo famous.

1. **RIHANNA AT THE MET BALL** face. It's not your typical resting bitch face (**RBF**). It's engaged-and-active bitch face.

2. A toothy **MISS AMERICANA PUSSY SPORTSWEAR CATALOG SMILE** is always in fashion. Think Chrissy Teigen. Determining what face you should make by where the camera is can be advantageous, too. I like to hide my big chin behind someone's shoulder when taking a selfie with them.

3. **PORNO PRODUCE AISLE** look is like you're seeing if the peaches are firm enough, but it also conveys you might want someone to get firm cuz of your peaches. Speaking of fruits, you may wanna try saying "Prune" as you pose. It's rumored the Olsens used to do it, but who knows? Just say I taught you. Saying

SUCK LESS AT SOUNDS

TRACKS TO MAKE YOU FEEL AS GOOD AS YOU LOOK

These are some of my favorite tracks to twirl to. My personal tunemaster, DJ Pastabody, would throw them on during a photo shoot or when we were getting ready to go out. This playlist will let the neighbors know that your pussy tastes just like Pepsi-Cola.

"Heartbreaker" *Mariah Carey featuring Jay-Z*

"Hypnotize" *The Notorious B.I.G.*

"Tom's Diner" *Suzanne Vega*

"Click Clack (Make Dat Money)" *RuPaul*

"Love Me Like You" *Little Mix*

"I'm Too Sexy" *Right Said Fred*

"Love Yourself" *Justin Bieber*

"All Night (Don't Stop)" *Janet Jackson*

"Too Funky" *George Michael*

"Do It Well" *JLo*

"Fembot" *Robyn*

"Don't Make Me Wait" *Jazmine Sullivan*

"Party in the USA" *Miley Cyrus*

"Break Free" *Ariana Grande featuring Zedd*

"Ignition (Remix)" *R. Kelly*

"Right on Time" *JoJo*

"Little Bird" *Annie Lennox*

"Do It to It" *Cherish featuring Sean P.*

"Queen" *Xelle featuring Mimi Infurst*

"Love Sex Magic" *Ciara featuring Justin Timberlake*

"Blow" *Beyoncé*

"Biscuit" *Ivy Levan*

"Crazy Bitch" *Buckcherry*

"How Will I Know" *Whitney Houston*

"When I Get You Alone" *Robin Thicke*

"Are You That Somebody" *Aaliyah*

"Pocketbook" *Me'Shell N'degéocello featuring Redman and Tweet*

"Walk It Out" *Jennifer Hudson featuring Timbaland*

"Prune" gives the perfect amount of puff and release without veering into duckface zone. Try it now. *Pruuune*. I bet you spit a little.

Certain proportions should be met either in real life or in your postproduction to make up what one would call a "good figure." For guys, your biceps should be double the size of your wrists. Rolling sleeves up to give the illusion of broader shoulders is a great way to make your waist look more tapered if you don't happen to be the ideal shape. Hooking your thumbs in your back pockets also gives that good V'd look. Monochromatic dressing is helpful to make a bitch look lean and make stretching you in Photoshop without distortion easier later. What else? Oh…cock rings. They can go around your whole package, around your balls only, or in a figure eight around your balls and dick. Whatever works for you. Hell, throw a plug in if it helps. If you're taking a selfie in the bathroom, *please* crop out that crapper or at least close the goddamn toilet seat.

WAYS TO MAKE YOUR DICK LOOK BIGGER

▓ *Wear button-fly jeans and don't fasten the second button from the bottom. Instabulge but not enough that it won't show there's a button undone.*

▓ *Photoshop.*

▓ *Wear underwear with shelfing pouches like the kind Francois Sagat makes. Cheapundies.com has some good ones, too.*

▓ *Take a condom and break through the end and put it around your cock and balls. Like an underwire bra aka the poor man's cock ring.*

▓ *Fuck people with smaller hands.*

If you're trying to look feminine, the correct camera placement can do most of the work. The most flaw-prone areas can be captured when the camera is below a girl (hips, double chin, brow ridge). Placing the camera a little above is always the smart way to go if you don't have time for surgery or tons of digital post work. When Eddie Redmayne was shooting his **trahnz** scenes in *The Danish Girl*, the cinematographer always ensured the frame was one to two inches higher than normal to make for a more feminine view of his face. I always do the same thing, because from below my chin looks like a Mount Rushmore with bronzer.

When all these tips fail, another way to look better is to take group shots with uglier people. The best way to come out looking good in a group-shot selfie is to hold the camera. When that's not an option, find whoever looks the worst and stand next to them. Buying your friends Fireball shots

and then saying "Selfie!" ten minutes later is a surefire way to shine. If you're worried you're going to be the worst one in the pic, that's when you make a funny face or find a large decorative urn to hide halfway behind. Props always help. If you can't get your hands on anything, post that ass up on the wall and put your shoulders forward. Boom. Standing centerfold. If you're not sure what to do with your hands while standing, the Susan Lucci trick works for all genders: Put your palms on your legs and press down lightly. It expands your chest, lowers your shoulders, and makes you look just better in general. You can even try it with your hands in your pockets. Put the book down and try it. Did you do it? Do it, seriously. I bet you think you're fancy now, huh? Ha-ha-ha. Idiot.

Just kidding. You're not an idiot, but y'know who is? That one person who thinks they should be in the group shot when you know you're just

gonna crop their ass anyway. Usually, I'm the person to go "No, no, this is one with the girls," trying to be nice about it, but sometimes it doesn't work. Like, if you're in a room full of queens and you have your genitals in a normal place, that means you shouldn't be in the picture. At least not all of them. In fact, how 'bout you actually take the pic for us? Thank you. Be a gentleman. That's what I wanted to say in the next shots, but as it was happening, I was like "Fuck this. I'mma put this in the book and use it as a learning experience."

As you can see (inset), he had given his camera to the guy I gave mine to and we all got just about the same pics. He posted this one. There's shadows on a few faces, nobody looks quite ready, and I look like I'm in the process of deciding how to tell this kid to get his fuckin' hand outta my wig. But Mr. Blue Man in the middle looks great.

So after I saw what he posted, I went "Okaaaaay..." in my head exactly how Delta Work would and went ahead with posting the one in which the majority of the group looked good... minus Ravey Smurf. (above)

That's how social media works. I'm not going to reblog a picture if I look like I've got a load on my tongue I don't wanna swallow. Candis was the host of the show and you can't even see her. Jesus. Group selfie decorum, man. Don't try to outpose each other. A solo pose in a group shot takes up too much room, so interact with the others in the shot. You put your hand upon your hip, and you make *you* look like shit. You put your hand upon *my* hip, then I dip, you dip, we dip. Engage. Model. Yes… *Yaaaas*… Oh, wait. Same thing, but chin down. We don't ever need to see up your nostrils.

Now, very few people will actually get to walk down a red carpet in Cannes or a runway during New York Fashion Week. I'm really lucky (that Courtney Act was already booked and I got to fill in) to have done a few of these ego-tripping strolls.

But understanding what makes press-hungry socio-paths like me tick could be just the ticket to getting into their squad or maybe cleaning their fluids off your couch. A model is like a prostitute with a chip on their shoulder. They usually want to be the most *most* person in any equation, and that includes sex. I'd much rather be worshipped by a normal person than fucked by a guy who I'm worried might think I look fat on my back. If you like dick way more than reading, keep going. I'm about to get to the good stuff. Like how you can use the red eye filter to make your hole pics look better.

THINGS THAT CAN ALWAYS BE LIGHTER, AKA THE HAUS OF DOLEZAL CHECKLIST

Birth weights. *Don't go crazy and smoke the trimesters away, but there is no need to gain more than 50 pounds for a pregnancy. It's a baby, not a litter.*

Your butthole. *Maybe make sure it doesn't look like a Brillo pad? Buttholes are like mood rings and can change all different shades, but it's up to you to make sure yours falls in the acceptable range between skin color and the shade of a new recess kickball.*

Your teeth. *When I got veneers I told them to make them two shades darker than they wanted to because I knew smoking, drinking, and assorted straight West Coasting was gonna discolor them anyway within a few years. I recommend the same for anyone who is fuckin' with their chompers.*

Your dog's fur. *Any dog that has a white face and has its fur around its eyes stained with that weird gray eye boogie seepage needs help. Arms of an Angel the animal if you don't wanna care for it and keep it cute. The easiest time to clean eye boogies is when they're lying down. Ambush them with a moist paper towel. They won't like it. It's like trying to put a Q-tip in a drag queen's ear during her number. But it'll save you having to Facetune their fur lighter in pics, too.*

How to SUCK LESS at GETTING FAMOUS/ INFAMOUS

Let's talk freely for a moment. These are just a few lessons you'll learn if you're a guy trying to make it in the big city. Girls have it easier, because getting big tits is easier than getting a big dick. Both are considered money in the bank for any kind of career as an ingenue or ingedude. When some early twenties person from nowheresville asks if I have any advice on where to find auditions or how to break into acting, I tell them if you can't figure out on your own how to audition, you're probably not cut out for it. I try to put on sunglasses as I say that last part so they know I'm an actual cunt and I don't just play one on TV. F'real. Think how many try and, out of those many, how many actually make it. I sure didn't despite having done everything other than rodeo and porn. I've never been a series regular, and my name is usually spelled wrong in my contracts. (If it's incorrect in actual credits on a SAG production, I get more money. Cool, huh?) Despite some *Nip/Tuck*ing and being on a couple of billboards, I never caught on until I made a mess on a game show. I came to LA to act, but didn't even make has-been. I'm a never-was.

But getting to the top of the fame game is a race to the bottom, and there's no bigger bottom than me. So when the World of Wonder told me I was hired for *RuPaul's Drag Race*, I knew I had a limited time to make as big of an impact as possible. I went in with a plan: specifically, either to fuck my way to the middle or to fuck everyone else up. I executed an almost textbook example of the old drag phrase "pulling the pag." Being disqualified may have made me slightly notorious, but I credit a lot of hard work along with hundreds of pounds of hair, makeup, and tape for truly making me a "thing." Because at thirty I knew my asshole wasn't getting any tighter and big breaks rarely come after a decade of obscurity. Unscripted television is really just a springboard for whatever you want to brand yourself as. Most people figuratively jump off that springboard and are like "Ooooh, this water is lovely" and float up to the pool bar. If I were lifeguarding, I'd yell, "Do laps, bitch. *Swim*. It's time to work." Say yes to everything. Because you don't want to swim back to your hometown with your tail between your legs.

People say, "How do you do that in heels?" and I simply tell them they should see what else I can do in them.

Not knowing what you want to do shouldn't stop you. I mean it's helpful. Figure out what general area you want to excel in or else it's like planning to win an Olympic medal because you know it'll look cute with an outfit once you get a sex change two decades later...kinda. Knowing where you want to go without knowing how to get there is fine. You'll meet people to help along the way (sometimes for money). Setting realistic general goals is key. Don't be just a "model." Be a "personality." No one has ever said "I want to grow up to be an Andrew Christian model" at career day mainly because even at junior high age, it doesn't exactly scream 401(k).

While we're on the subject, if you say you're a model but the closest thing to an agency representing you is Instagram, what you actually are is a liarmouth. But then again, many reality shows fib, too. *RuPaul's Drag Race*, for instance, purports to find America's Next Drag Superstar in the same way that *America's Next Top Model* said they were gonna find the next top supermodel. Sure, reality shows find superstars, but does anyone remember who won *American Idol* when Jennifer Hudson lost? I sure don't. My friend Tracy said *RuPaul's Drag Race* claims to be the Olympics of drag when in reality it's the Rock-Paper-Scissors of drag. They get it wrong more often than they get it right. #FACT.

Since we're on the subject of lies, now is a good time to get further into the *why* of reality shows. In your hometown, growing up, probably any girl who dated eighteen different dudes at once was referred to as a skank. Now we refer to her as ABC's *Bachelorette*. You won't be shocked to know that in eight seasons of *RuPaul's Drag Race*, Pisces, Cancers, and Sagittariuses showed up with the most frequency because those signs frequently are emotional and like attention. (Other notable reality Cancers, besides me: Bianca Del Rio, Jujubee, Bob, Milk, Big Ang, Mike Tyson, Fantasia, Michael Phelps—all *big* personalities.)

Reality television appearances are basically notoriety nachos: They won't fill you up like dinners full of fame—and you need a meal. Specifically, a meal ticket. To get these paid gigs, try working to brand yourself by aligning with causes and opportunities that cater to you and your audience. For instance, I enjoy bareback sex, so I speak openly about Truvada and PrEP in hopes I'll get a deal. I also fucked a guy with psoriasis once, so I'm also all about chemical-free skin products, like those that I endorse for Obsessive Compulsive Cosmetics. (See what I did there?) What I'm trying to say is stay current and stay cunt. Priority one after any big event that's considered a star-making opportunity is to keep your visibility up. Many take that too literally and say yes to every free drink, thereby increasing their body's square footage and, literally, their visibility. Don't do that. A lotta girls come off the game show and

*Everyone here has been on some sorta reality/
unscripted programming, has been in someone
who was, and/or both.*

within the first year they have a RuPork's Drag
Face mug from all the cocktailing combined with
water retention from flying and coke bloat.

This all must sound/look like a *lot* of legwork
(depending on whether you're reading it or listen-
ing to the audiobook). While I was writing this,
I had to turn down invitations to an Elton John
party from my friend David and a weekend in the
Keys with a redheaded man who lets me count
the freckles on his asshole with my tongue. That
alone shows you how dedicated I was to educating
and makes it impossible to deny my work ethic.

If you're not ready to work that hard and make
serious sacrifices like me, maybe it's time to defer
those dreams. Drown that kitten that was you on
the A-list party invites and cozy up to the idea of
being a plus one. The easiest way to get there is
by being so good at sex that a hookup wifes you
up. Look at Amber Rose. She went to high school
across the street from my house in Philly with my
cousin and was a bitch who got her ass beat by
my friend Tank Ass. Li'l bit of Kanye cum and
Wiz jizz later, she's basically made it. I'm looking forward to seeing who the father of her next
abortion will be. I bet she could give some tips
on where to find a man (Source Awards), but I'd
say try turning on your favorite hookup app in an
area with really good real estate, a yacht club, or a
medical school. Word to the wise: once you get in
a trick's house, don't go opening closets or snoop-
ing. I had cameras all over my last house and saw
lots of people where they didn't belong.

Speaking of closets, my buddy who dated a
boy-bander sure did keep the guy's secret, but he
also kept that guy's Teen Choice Award (which is
a full-size surfboard). Like, how the fuck do you
explain that? The guy shouldn't have been getting
any awards anyway since he was playing scaredy-
closet-cat, so in this case, I say good. But under
normal circumstances, the only things that are
acceptable to steal from rich people you fuck are
hearts and Netflix passwords. I wish you all the
success you can swallow.

POP-UP QUIZ!
ARE YOU RIGHT FOR
A REALITY SHOW?
FIND OUT HERE:

If you were to go on a competition-based reality game show, it'd be because

    ❏ A. you're looking to set a good example for your community.

    ❏ B. you're a masochist, an egomaniac, and a failure at your chosen profession.

    ❏ C. production waived the piss test and a check's a check.

    ❏ D. all of the above.

The kind of show you'd want to be on would probably

    ❏ A. tell the contestants lies about each other to create tension.

    ❏ B. pay their staff salaries that, after taxes and divided by the sixty hours a week they worked, come out to be less than minimum wage and thereby technically illegal.

    ❏ C. allow participants in recovery to call their sponsors once a week but keep them motivated with Muhammed Ali pics and inspirational posters for the hotel room walls.

    ❏ D. all the above since these are pretty much standard in reality television.

If at any point you knew you weren't going to win, you would try to get the boot by

    ❏ A. defecating in a large pot and aggressively stirring it by telling another contestant that you violated rules knowing they would cry foul.

    ❏ B. complaining that a female producer was only smoking out contestants she adored and not you.

    ❏ C. refusing to get into a van at ten p.m. after a fourteen-hour day and after being handed $75.00 for you and eleven other contestants to eat ($6.25 each).

    ❏ D. doing exactly what they told you to do when they hired you.

If you were to have a married executive producer's dick in you during production, something you might say to them in the future would be

    ❏ A. "I sucked your dick from the back, raw-dogged AND kept my mouth shut about it, and you're gonna act like how your work buddies try to treat me and others is OK?"

    ❏ B. "You can save those pearl necklaces for another cocktestant of yours who showed me *all* those texts and pics you sent him."

    ❏ C. "How is it you have the backbone of a scoliosis patient when it comes to doing what's right but you're able to support that two-hander of a cock?"

    ❏ D. "You're wearing a condom next time."

If you were looking for things to complain about to the host, you'd probably say

- ❑ A. nothing because they couldn't hear it over the lines they're being fed through their earpiece.
- ❑ B. nothing because you were told not to make eye contact or talk to the host unless directly engaged by the host.
- ❑ C. *"Bye."*
- ❑ D. "All the above."

If you were asked back to do another round of the same show, you would

- ❑ A. giggle.
- ❑ B. immediately jump at the chance, only to have said chance rescinded and be told later that it was a tactical move to show you who's boss by someone you were fucking who would know.
- ❑ C. have a lawyer review the contract in case it gave the production company 100 percent career control over all media, future works, and licensing.
- ❑ D. build a snowman in hell.

Your career path after your reality TV stint could best be described as

- ❑ A. setting fire to everybody's rain while shouting like a transvestite suffragette.
- ❑ B. an amateur arsonist with a focus on bridges.
- ❑ C. a constant gardener who knows that land mines grow best in light shade, especially when irrigated with a steady stream of piss and disdain.
- ❑ D. brunch shows and light escort work before doing another reality show.

If you selected mostly A's, that's cool. You should do *Cupcake Wars*.

If you selected mostly B's, you'd be perfect on Bravo... or bullshit. Same diff.

If you selected mostly C's, you've won a year's subscription to Instagram. Go to "Apps" on your phone and download it. You're welcome.

If you selected mostly D's, you will probably be on *Big Brother* at some point.

How to **SUCK LESS** around **FAMOUS PEOPLE**

'm not famous. I'm a novelty at best. Sometimes people say I'm gaymous. Meaning if you're gay, you probably know of me or know someone I tried to hook up with when I was performing at their local club. When I meet people, I can usually put them into one of two categories: people who will ask for a picture and people who won't. It's fine, asking for a picture. I love it. I mean I didn't get into this business because I was a shy wallflower who didn't love attention. But sometimes, if my war paint isn't on or if I'm just trying to enjoy a panini, it might be nice for you to do a quick boot 'n' scoot with me. Basically, tell me my boots are cute or give me props and then sorta scoot off. A great example: Katy Perry once hollered at me to sing "Boy Is a Bottom" midway through "Chow Down" at a party, yet I was still too shy to say anything to her until she was leaving. As she passed, KP purred approval at my shoes because she had the same ones in pink (Louboutin Pigalle Pensee). Compliments are the easiest icebreaker. As my fangirl flamed, I realized I should get a picture, but in all honesty, I was happy just feeling her shine and didn't wanna keep her from enjoying her night for

one second more since she had made mine. (FYI, I sure woulda sucked the hair off the balls of the sweet-looking man who was with her, who I won't name here.) I coulda tried to force a photo, but not everything in life needs to be calibrated later by how many likes or views it gets.

Like if you're at a show, don't stand in the front row of a show and film the whole time. Most performers would rather see faces if they are performing close enough to actual bodies. If you have a familiar-faced friend, never make them feel like every time is selfie time. They're your buddy, not a social media tool. When Alaska and I were backstage at the Queen show to see Adam, sure we were Glamberting out but the only celebrity we actually got a pic with was Lisa Rinna's lips (Lisa Rinna was also in the photo).

You may wanna grab a Swiffer, 'cause I'm about to drop a bunch more names.

I was lucky enough to work with Betty White twice in the past decade. I saw people jumping for pics with her and falling all over her. People got so worked up, they forgot that asking for pictures on set is tacky and unprofessional, especially when it involves asking the ninety-four-year-old national

Find us in the M4ET section of Craigslist.

Fill in the bubbles.

treasure to take it again because the flash wasn't on. Someone actually asked her to do a quick video. Decorum was out the window. Like, each person who asked knew damn well that Betty ain't got time for their nonunion bullshit.

My friend Todrick has Taylor Swift on his voice mail and that makes sense. Abuse the fuck outta her if you meet her. She'll let you. She's that type. Bitch'll probably walk your dog for you. But don't try that shit with me. Don't be asking me to call my friends with gold trophies so you can hear their voice mail. Yes, I have the CW's Hawkman's

number from when he used to go-go dance, but, no, we cannot call him to squawk.

Attempting to muster recognition from anyone you meet is also dicey. If a dude asks me "Do you remember meeting me at ____?" I say, "Yeah, you were that one guy." If he persists and starts to spill details of our singular encounter that is escaping me, I simply tell him, "I believe you." It's my nice way of saying "I'm sure it happened, but I sure as fuck don't remember." I'd rather be real than fake it and lamebrain out when someone comes at me the next time I'm in their town. Telling me who you know that I know won't always be a safe bet either. Like, sure. I fucked this one guy who was one of the child actors chucking rocks at Forrest Gump, but I don't feel the need to brag about it, y'know? His dick was probably what Forrest was running from, because it is fuckin' *huge*. (Hi, Todd!) See? I'm modest. But in reality, I was all like "Beat up this ass like you tried to beat Forrest."

I actually met the *Forrest Gump* fucker at a show. He was not a fan. He thought I was repulsive because I was fellating an audience member (because, amazing as it is, I had already watched Detox do her Mannequin number three hundred times in five years). And y'know what? The guy I was blowing ended up using the "Do you remember me" line the next year at the *same* club. Again, I said I believed him and he sure did pull up the picture of the back of my head in his crotch. He got the full Meet, Greet, and Skeet package. Usually it's just called a Meet and Greet. Not a Meet, Stay, and Tell Me About Your Cat You Named Willam but Then It Ran Away and Oh You're Thinking About Doing Drag but You're Also a Bipolar and You Give Me the Strength to Go On.

Fuckin' greet me and let me greet you back and then put the coin on the dresser and hit the door. At an M&G, you usually have about fifteen to twenty seconds of my attention as a given. No bathroom chatter or locker-room talk ever. Have some common sense. I ran into Leah Remini at a local med spa and took my own advice, simply saying *The King of Queens* was my eleven p.m. TBS jam and that I was there at our mutual friend Michelle Visage's recommendation. She was all like "Oooo…one of Michelle's girls? OK." I was happy at that point that she was even talking to me, because I mean we were in the lobby of a **pumping** parlor and it's not like we were there just to Zen out. Although I had just had an extensive Eastern medicine/meditation consultation (which means I thought so intensely about getting Botox into me that a nice Asian lady named Sharon came into the room and pumped me full of it).

Treating a famous person like a normal person is usually the best bet. Especially in bed. Don't ever mention when my dick is out that you think I shoulda won *Drag Race*, please. Think of it as **dickscretion**. For instance, I blew half the gay male leading cast of *Mean Girls* and, sure, technically that's only two people if you don't count Tim Meadows, but when I blew that one guy, I didn't post something stupid like "On Wednesdays, we suck dick" even though it was a Wednesday and it was my first starfuck. He told me not to talk about it, so I just wiped my mouth with some Burger King napkins from my glove box and went about the rest of my night. NBD.

A lot of people comment that they don't know what to say after they meet me or mention I'm intimidating. I would say sorry, but it's not my fault. There is no reason to be afraid of speaking to someone you're a fan of. Guess what?

I *never* get tired of hearing how much you love me. G'head. Bitch, I'll take the next train if you wanna talk and, *yes*, I will take that selfie with you. Never apologize for taking up my time. It actually takes up more of the alleged time that you're not actually sorry for taking up. If you ask someone for a moment of their time and apologize while you do it, why should they go along?

Penmanship is everything.

It's like saying "Ugh, this is horrible. Here, try it." Don't be sorry. Be resolute and direct. I won't say no to a picture unless I know I can't reasonably pull off my semi-sober face.

A Reddit user said I was a cunt at an M&G at American Apparel in NYC and then, in the same thread, another commenter tried to apologize for me without even having been present. They hypothesized that I was maybe having an off day or something because I wouldn't come around a table to take selfies with everyone. I was positioned in between Courtney and Alaska, and it woulda been impossible. Like, I gave out cupcakes to the end of the line at that very same event but totally lied about them being gluten-free. Call me terrible for that, but it's totally within a person's right to not interrupt their day to do your impromptu M&G exactly how you want it. Like, if I sign a picture with just my name and don't write a personalized haiku in my own blood, would that make someone say to never meet their idols? I dunno. There's a certain point when some people have to just give up pretending they want new friends instead of fans. I totally get that Gaga doesn't want to spend a whole day taking selfies to satisfy a few hundred when that time is more valuably used creating content the whole world will enjoy. Comparing myself to Gaga or Ru is about as far-fetched as using a Frisbee as a fuck toy, but I hope I've shed a little light on things. So let's recap: (1) Keep it cute, (2) keep it quick, (3) insert Yaaas/Fierce/Love, and (4) selfie and a send-off.

How to **SUCK LESS** at

TALKING TO TRAHNZ
(TWENTY DUMB DRAG QUESTIONS)

13

N o, I don't want to answer some questions for your college thesis on what gender roles play in modern society or what drag means to you. STFU. If you're paying money to learn and you're trying to write about drag, maybe consider a better-accredited facility.

Q: I want to start drag. What do I do?

A: Watch my tutorials and do the opposite. I'd say do stuff people will give money to see or stuff that's so awful they pay you to go away. Do as much drag as you can everywhere you can while you're still passionate about actually creating something. Do drag on the Internet, on game shows, at bus stations, at clubs, at churches, at Church's Chicken, at Shangela's house. Because if you don't end up making a name for yourself and succeeding (translation: being paid), it turns into a rather expensive hobby. If as a baby newbie queen, you're doing another performer's signature song as a tribute, homage, or straight-up jank, then you better turn it out and somehow make it not only different from your predecessor's but also better in some ways. If I see you lip-synching a song I've popularized in one of my live singing acts, I'm simply reminded that you're not as talented as I am. Find some way to dance the house down or get a gimmick real quick, because at a certain point, audiences go "OK…what's next?" I dunno what else to write advice-wise, but I will just shamelessly steal a Chad Michaels tip: don't be that queen with the dirty tights. Put a towel on the floor where you're getting dressed and clean off your feet with alcohol wipes before slipping them into some pumps. The alcohol wipes are handy, because sometimes after untucking, your basement smells like a basement. For a more pleasant ride home, give a quick swipe with a swab before getting in the car.

Q: Where do the balls go?

A: My favorite spot to hide balls is in my mouth. But if you want me to specifically talk tucking my balls, here goes. If you're just doing some quick drag in a loose garment,

I'm totally fine with advocating a lazy lady casserole and just pulling all your junk back between your legs like Buffalo Bill into what I call a monster mash (see Pearl Liason). Put a few pairs of tights on and make sure, with an honest friend or a good look in the mirror, that it looks like all your luggage is properly stowed in the underass compartment.

When a tighter tuck is required, for a more body-conscious look, that's when it's time to play hide your keister eggs and stuff 'em up your body. Guys, y'know how when you're on your back, about to jizz, and sometimes a ball pops up into the cavity above your dick and then you feel all emasculated even though there's already a dick in your ass? OK. Well, that's where I put my balls. I have to put my left ball up first, 'cause it's bigger. If I put the right one up first, the left one is all like "*Ocupado, señor.*" So, yeah. I get the balls up and then I pull my dick back and wrap my loose sack skin around it like a dirty breakfast burrito. Then you just need to keep it in place with a gaff (a super-tight thong-string combo) or a few strips of tape. When taping, I like to dip into it so I don't get any thigh skin or extra cheek fat in there. Otherwise it leaves stretch mark–like underskin crease bruises, like when you carry a bag that's too heavy in the crook of your elbow.

3 **Q:** Wait. So you actually put tape on your balls?
A: Yes. The fuck I'm supposed to use? Post-Its? (You can also purchase a roll of my Tuct Tape on my website www.willambelli.com. New: $10. Used: $50.)

4 **Q:** How do you get the sticky stuff off?
A: Your father. In actuality, you're right to query. It can get sticky down there when your father doesn't thoroughly get at my balls like a hungry buttmunch. That's when you break out the ol' Goo Gone for one of the uses As Not Seen on TV. Just smear a little around. My friend Courtney says I'm gonna get taint cancer from it, but it's got orange oil in it so it can't be that bad. That being said, you can always use coconut oil, too. She uses that. Either way, it is mutually agreed upon that you should get the sticky stuff off

Ballwatch. Can you see the little dent created when I shove two round balls up into my otherwise taut stomach? Fuckin' pervert. Turn the goddamn page.

with a remover of some sort before trying to do it in the shower or else it'll roll up like wet semen (any guy who's ever jerked off in the shower knows what I'm talking about).

5

Q: Wait. So where are your balls?

A: On either side of that dent above my panties on page 65. Guys with big dicks don't have trouble tucking. Guys with big balls do 'cause they get shoved up into the body. I'm like a Hungry Man meal. Small portion of meat but a lotta potato. Y'know when your mom used to yell at you to get in the car? I do that with my balls all the time. A nice hot shower helps them hang low and get them ready to launch off to taint land.

6

Q: Does it hurt to sit down?

A: Only if there's no lube or money.

7

Q: I want to do drag, but I don't have any money.

A: Remember this: long bangs, heavy powder, head down, walk fast, no spook. Let me break it down: "Long bangs" means you don't have to worry about how your wig is glued to your forehead or if it's in the right spot or, hell, even covering your brows. "Heavy powder" means turn your face into an imperfection-free mask. Suffocate the man who lurks beneath with a dust storm of coverage that will last till his beard peeks back through. "Head down" means to remember in photos to keep your head down. Look right above the flash so your eyes seem up and open. "Walk fast" means…well, walk fast. A rock in motion tends to stay in motion. While you're not a rock, if it's your first time in drag, you

Hungry Trahnz: all potato, no meat.

66

just might be a **brick**. So keep making laps and avoid pools of unfortunate lighting. No blue! "No spook" means just that: "to spook" means to garner attention because your look is scary or noticeable. Thank you Krystal Summers for this wise advice.

8 Q: How'd you get into that?

A: We have tricks. Here's one now:

Bangles don't fit past those man knuckles? No problem.

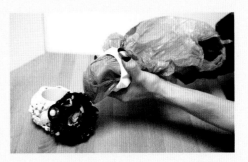

A plastic bag over your hand will allow you to slip your hand through the bangles without tearing the skin off.

Shave your arms too, while you're at it. Fuckin' beast.

Wrap thread around your fingers to slide off rings that got too tight from all the water weight you've gained cocktailing.

9 Q: Any tips for me?

A: Be as nice as Ongina, as daring as Divine, as sickening as Mayhem, as take-no-shit as Delta, as chill as The Princess, and as unsinkable as Rhea Litre. Know your herstory and not just queens from TV. Jackie Beat, Christeene, the Cockettes. Try to have fun...and safety pins. Some bitch will always need one. Oh and when in doubt, just think "What would Raja do?"

10

Q: When did you know you wanted to be a woman?

A: I don't want to be a woman. But if I ever transition, I want to be so passable that I can believably call in sick at work due to complications stemming from an abortion blood fart.

11

Q: I love drag queens, but I don't wanna go alone/I'm not out/I'm lame.

A: You're never alone with alcohol on your side. The ghosts of bad decisions past are all around you and will guide you. It's not hard. What have you got to lose? I try to look at every new face I meet as a potential new seat, and anyone who doesn't do the same is bound to miss out on some shit. Just try it. It's not prom.

12

Q: What's RuPaul like?

A: I'm not familiar with his dietary restrictions.

13

Q: What happens if you get hard in drag?

A: I double my booking fee. You ever see that part in *Alice in Wonderland* after she ate that acid cupcake and outgrew that house? You star in a one-man show called *Tuck Neverlasting*.

14

Q: Will you do my makeup?

A: Why Yes! Yes, I will random stranger who smells of whiskey in the club. But I need you to put your shoes back on and stop yelling at every girl onstage to do Beyoncé. This is not Spotify. You don't get to pick what we do. Now, what's your PIN?

15

Q: Why are you such a bitch?

A: Well, dear, I work at a place where people come to get fucked up because it's more fun there than wherever you probably go to make money. So, for me, it's like being a Muppet in a Holocaust film. Sure, it's fun to have a gig and be in everyone's splash zone, but let's see you keep a whale in a fishtank and calibrate your mood. Free Willy, bitch.

16

Q: If I were straight, I'd bang you in drag...

A: Oh wow. *Thank you!* BTW, if Christmas were in July, you'd still be an asshole. That's right outta *The Notebook*, isn't it?

17 **Q:** Can I try on your wig?

A: Can you? Possibly. Will you? Only if you fuck it offa me.

18 **Q:** What's my drag name?

A: Well, I got my moniker because my dad fucked my mom and that's what they named me. You don't need a drag name. Some of the best in the business don't change theirs (Boy George, Charles Busch, Kevin Aviance, Joey Arias, Mathu Andersen, Leigh Bowery, Willi Ninja), but if you really feel the need to, please don't use the whole middle name and pet way of working it out.

Best/worst names IMHO: Amnesty Barrel, Karen from Finance, Rape Soda, Raquel Felch, Crystal Beth Ann Fettermean, Bunny St. Blowclouds, Frittata Jenkins, Mrs. Peaches von Tiffanysworth, and the classic Helluva Bottom Carter.

19 **Q:** Shouldn't you be in the men's room?

A: Call me Caitlyn, cunt.

20 **Q: What did you do on *RuPaul's Drag Race*?**

A: I actually get this question a lot and treasure it more each time. When I was disqualified, I was at Toad Hall in SF and listened to the bar all laugh when something funny happened and yell support when Latrice and I won. But when RuPaul sent me home, the entire bar gasped at the same time, and it was as unnatural as hearing a whole room fart in unison. Everyone looked at me, wanting answers…and I *loved* it! So giving up all the mystery of what I actually did would be too easy. It's almost as easy as getting Alyssa to guest edit this next part on figuring out how to tongue pop.

Every magical tongue pop must include a moist mouth; a strong, very flexible, well-trained tongue; and discipline. Place your tongue on the roof of your mouth and imagine the sound echoing through hallways, and when the moment is right, pull back and release the pop of life!
And I thank you.
Always and forever,
Alyssa Edwards

How to **SUCK LESS** at **STYLE**

14

Isaac Mizrahi said, "A girl can do and say anything she wants when she looks like a lady." I think this is super true. I always try to dress for the station or job in life where I want to be, regardless of where I actually am. Like, usually I dress like an unemployed Powerball winner in all vintage and a nice watch. Some bitch ain't giving you **nooch** in a store? Flash a little wrist and show the shopgirl the T. As a kid, I said no to being an altar boy because (get this) I didn't want to wear a dress. That garment they tried to make me wear woulda given me all the curves of a refrigerator, and I wouldn't have stood a chance of getting molested.

As an adult, I get to wear whatever I want. I fought with my nephew Levi when he was five and said I dressed like a girl because I had long hair and earrings. I told him boys could dress like that too and pulled up a Jack Sparrow pic on my phone. It's so satisfying winning a fight with a child. He has since learned I also wear dresses, but he knows enough not to call them ladies' dresses. I wear *my* dresses. A dress is a dress is a tunic is a robe. Men have worn dress-like garments for most of the world's history, and only recently have they

been scrutinized for it. I take off my clothes more times in a night than some do in a full week, but as long as the presentation is perfect, you can get away with anything that may raise an eyebrow. Never be bare legged. Some Body Bling or Sally Hansen Airbrush Spray Makeup or even some skin-toned Capezio fishnets will save you lots of filtering later.

One of the biggest mistakes I see with hose-wearers is not wearing panties. The answer is *yes*. I usually wear a light panty over tights. If you're wearing fishnets, a panty patch may suffice. If a woman wears fishnet panty hose with nothing under them, her vagina will look like a defrosted piece of salmon casually flung onto a chain-link fence. It's not cute. My balls and dick skin trying to squeeze through diamond-patterned fishnet openings like genital-colored Play-Doh is something an audience never needs to see twice.

Your foundation garments are key in presenting a good overall look. No one should know what's going on under your clothes. A jockstrap or cute bra peeking out is fine, but anything waist-bandy that forces a muffin top or back roll is never the look. If you're doing a shaper garment

WILLAM

Don't be afraid of scissors. Definitely check out some tutorials on YouTube though first, because you don't wanna look like you lost a fight with one of those Project Runway *faggots. (Hi, Blake and Josh!)*

or Spanx, it happens often. Conceal it maybe with a belt or just take it the fuck off. Underclothes are stupid. Are you fucking Amish? No.

Here's your getting-dressed checklist:

❑ Will someone fuck you?

❑ Will this look good on someone else's floor later?

❑ Can you put this on in thirty seconds to get out of that person's house?

❑ What if you died? This would be your ghost outfit for the rest of eternity, and you don't wanna be known as that Old Navy ghost, do you?

❑ Can you run from the police in your outfit? Never wear something you can't run from someone in…

❑ …including heels. You should be able to do anything in heels that you can do in flats other than fuck. Ain't nobody never told no one to keep their Tory Burchs on while they fucked. It's called knocking boots for a reason—and correct me if I'm wrong, but I think the term is "fuck-me pump," not "fuck-me flat."

Since I already dropped one label name, I'll keep it going. I love nice things but am not

The lady who can afford Louboutins does not do her own nails. So this Louboutin nail polish is only good for one thing: touch-ups on my pumps.

so much a shopper. My mom actually went into labor with me while shopping at Kmart, which was basically me trying to get outta that crappy store by any means necessary even if it meant escaping her womb. I love secondhand and consignment shops. More than 75 percent of my book looks are seconhand, and I will happily give you outfit details if you tweet me questions with #SuckLess. There are pretty dope flea markets in LA, like the Fairfax High School one or the massive one at the Rose Bowl weekly. If you know what you're looking for, they're easier to tackle. Bring lots of small bills in easy denominations and always offer 20 to 30 percent less than what you actually want to pay for the item. A counter-offer from the salesperson will usually yield a better price. Be careful of knockoffs and fakes at any online or resale vendor. The only knockoff I've ever owned is a computer case from a backroom flea market in Dubai. I had to go up three staircases and through a closet to get to a room that had all the best fakes I've ever seen. Many knock-offs can be almost convincing because they're made right alongside the mass-produced real items in Asia or India. The way French labels like Vuitton and Hermès get away with saying "Made in France" is by applying the finishing touches in their home country, like the hardware. I'm sure that's true in some cases and false in others, but my Dubai fake fooled the Vuitton store in Beverly Hills when I went in to get it monogrammed.

One thing that's definitely real is the savings from buying secondhand. I got this Chanel suit for four hundred dollars in London, and although it was a bit mother-of-the-bride once I saw how my ass looked in the pants, I was dead set on transforming it. 'Member that episode of *The Simpsons* when Marge finds the Chanel suit, gets into a country club because of her style, but then has to

keep altering it so the ladies who lunch won't think she's poor? Necessity breeds invention, and, no, that's not a barebacking joke.

While my day-to-day garb is mostly work pants, Timbs, and a tee, my drag is even more

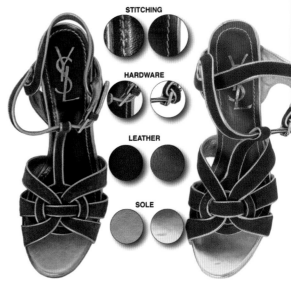

Can you tell which is real and which is fake? Look for details like stitching, the overall line of the shoe and attention to detailing. Tweet me and I'll tell you the answer @willam.

concise. I instated a rule that everything I buy has to fall into one of three categories, because mixing separates is the best way to create new looks without spending money:

1. **LUXE.** Like a rich bitch (Miss Piggy with a coke problem).
2. **CLOWN-LIKE.** Something with whimsy or irony (Carol Burnett or Aileen Wuornos).
3. **WHORE.** *But* think whore in the back of Eddie Murphy's limo, not Bunny Ranch budget puss.

Two pieces that were hard to wear individually turned into four pieces that look great with anything. Yes, I'm counting the hair bow. I mean it's Chanel, technically.

Look good if your friends look good.

If you love something but are having a hard time heading to the register with it, ask yourself how your style icons would wear it. Is it Audrey Hepburn or is it Jennifer Love Hewitt in a TV biopic about Audrey? Is it effortless rock god or is it closer to some shit rhinestoned Ed Hardy? If you lust for it but don't know how it would look right with your current wardrobe, it's tantamount to buying art that you really like but it totally won't go with everything else in your house. Don't buy for just the high. Walk away and come back to it. You don't wanna spend time obsessing over an outfit. You wanna spend time having fun in it and then wearing it home inside out. It's always good to have what I call a little turnting garment a.k.a. a **chicken bucket dress**. It's something that (a) makes people wanna have sex with you and (b) is not precious in the least, and you can easily move around the stick shift to get your head down or ass up.

We've all been there when a friend is trying on an outfit and they like it even though it's not so hot on them. If someone's got too much going on, I'll just say something like "That is a lot of look." But only if they ask. People know that there's a seed of truth in every joke. When going out in a group or meeting up, looking like you all are going to the same event is key. You don't need to

If you like to wear *black or white to a club, take special care. Club lighting will highlight any kinda flakeage or dandruff you may not even know you have. Make sure them whites are fresh too, because that Shout pen can't compete with a black light.*

look like Tina Knowles styled you, but you want to be able to get into the same parties in case there is a dress code or footwear restriction. Look good if your friends look good.

If your clique has someone whose dress code is always a mess code, cut that shit out like a tumor. Try the whole "Are you gonna get ready?" routine, like you couldn't fathom them possibly going out in that outfit. If the passive-aggressive joking doesn't work, a direct approach might be nec-essary. Some may counter by talking about how Mother Teresa had, like, one dress or they'll go "I don't care what I wear or what people think." Set them straight. Inform them that shabby chic is for houses, not people, and they can stay home and count commercials. My friends know that if they don't wanna help our group look cute in our self-ies, they should go away, or at least buy us enough beer that we don't care that they look like a hobo. Stay…but pay.

10 FAVORITE THRIFT STORES

*C*all them consignment or resale or whatever. Point is, somebody had their stank on it first so clean it or crash on with your bad self. Just Google them for the address. My word count was too high.

1. London: Rellik–*all the names you love like McQueen, Alaia, Hermes, etc.*

2. Toyko: Vivienne Westwood Closet Child–*a resale store full of ALL Westwood.*

3. Beverly Hills: Paper Bag Princess—*where old Hollywood goes to sell archival-worthy pieces with a really cool toilet.*

4. San Francisco: Helpers House of Couture—*This appointment only spot is run by a spitfire Tom Ford-clad fashionista named Joy Bianchi with all proceeds going to the mentally-handicapped. Worth a look.*

5. Dallas: Dolly Python—*A southern-fried emporium of vintage*

6. Sydney: Zoo Emporium—*my cover dress is an old beaded dress I go from here and had made-over. Quality shit.*

7. Chicago: Beatnik's—*Can't quite tell you what this store specializes in but I'd say if Norman Bates wanted to crossdress poptastically, he could shop here. Solid mid-western wear and trendy stuff.*

8. Hollywood: Wasteland—*Where fashion fags go to sell their stuff so it's very current. But don't buy any Herve Leger dresses there. They're all fakes.*

9. Philadelphia: Philly AIDS Thrift—*Any AIDS thrift store usually has great stuff since it's where most gay goodies go. Raja nabbed the bangles from page 67 from Out of the Closet in LA when Holly Woodlawn's wardrobe was sent there (RIP).*

10. Anywhere: WycoVintage.com & Defunkd.com—*vintage rock t-shirt heaven.*

How to **SUCK LESS** at

HAVING A
GREAT BODY

That's me trying to smile while sucking in my double chin in fifth grade. When we passed around our yearbooks to get signed the last day of class, mine came back with "Thar he blows" written under it. Sure, I was insulted. The only problem was, I didn't know if my rude class-mates were using *Moby-Dick* quotes because I was fat or because word had spread about how I got mono. (Hi, James!)

Either way, after that, I vowed to be in control of the one thing I could control in my life: *exactly* what goes into and comes out of my body. It's one of the reasons actors and models obsess over their looks so much. It's the one thing they can actually control, and oftentimes it dictates their daily lives.

I know my advice is rather blunt: Get in shape. It's the best gift you can give yourself. If you stop eating processed crap and start cook-ing, it'll help you feel like you're doing at least one thing in your life every day for the good of your longevity. It's harder for people who aren't cookie cutters to make it, so try your best to eliminate variables that could cause you not to book work. Being called "skinny fat" to my face by my first

agent was a wake-up call. He said if I couldn't take my shirt off during pilot season, he didn't want to represent me. It's THAT cutthroat out here. That's when I started doing some squats or crunches every time I wanted to eat something. It's part of an actor's job to disappear into a part, and extra weight held me back.

The good thing is, whenever I diet, I become an utter skank, because if I eat really clean, it's easier to clean out my body for visiting dicks. I'm not saying being Paleo is a replacement for douch-ing, but sometimes when I have the right balance of food in a day, I can pinch off a loaf and not even worry about putting unwanted toppings on another guy's hot dog (side note: nobody wants sauerkraut). Don't be scared, though. Sometimes when you fast or starve yourself, your body kinda goes into a battery-save mode that makes your brain operate a little slower. You more easily get mad (that's your blood sugar dipping) and you might start to get a little *Still Alice*, forgetting shit. It's fine. Your brain is just on low speed since you're not supplying it with enough fuel to run. The good thing is, it makes you feel real damn Zen and is spiritually cleansing. The other good thing is, since you won't be filling up with all them groceries, you can spend your money on important things that will make it easier for you to like you, like drugs (if you drink, know that lighter-colored liquors tend to be less nutritionally damning calorie-wise). There are specific times when being fat can't be avoided, like if you're transitioning from man to woman. Estrogen usually makes a girl put on some weight, and that's fine. The extra pounds soften all the manly, hard angles of a face. And, hell, if you wanna keep eating, g'head. If you get a gut, you can at least forgo tucking, because no one will be able to see if you have a cock or not. There are a whole buncha men and women who are attracted soley to big girls too, probably because no matter where you grab them, it feels like boobs.

Many want big, fat asses. Most drag queens in Florida, where I came of age, **pump** to achieve an hourglass figure. It could be because it's too hot to pad down in that climate. They're sweating their fucking mugs off already, so sticking a couch and a half onto their actual love-seat area is just asking for heatstroke. I decided to do it the old-fashioned way. Squats, hiking, and taking every set of stairs I see helps. I also love donkey kicks, lateral leg raises, and leg presses. Combine those with wearing heels and dancing around at work, and my ass is pretty solid. It's not hard to put on some music and dance around till you're sweaty. I like to get high and then do cardio. Pop that pussy

so severely that you give yourself an episiotomy (that's when a lady's pussy tears while birthing—you're welcome).

"If ya can't tone it, tan it" was my default mode when I was heavier. I've been that lazy fucker who rationalizes going to tan instead of going to the gym. For some months I also called my gym dues my swim club dues because I was going to the gym just to use the spa. Decide if you have a gym membership or a hot tub membership. Seriously. And while you're there, don't use the shower gels provided. The only thing that stuff's

Supplements are great but can be tricky. A cycle or two is cool but may increase chances of cancer, hair loss, and fucked up skin. Imagine putting your hands on someone's back and feeling one of those big cystic bad boys popping. I can't deal with whiteheads on my man. Not even doggy. No, sir. A pimply back is no contender for this transgender.

Keep your head down so you don't strain your neck. My wig was gonna fall off otherwise.

good for is making your urethra burn when you play hand sandwich with that freeballer in basketball shorts once you stalk him to the shower. The gym is a great spot to make new friends—like freeballer fag—and an even better spot to bring existing friends you want to see naked. Plus, establishing workout dates with anyone keeps you accountable so you actually show up. Smaller, casual group hikes or adult sport leagues, like dodgeball and kickball, are awesome, too. The gay basketball group LambdaBasketball.com has so many hot guys that I would pretend to text and take slo-mo videos of guys doing jump shots. I was the entertainment one year at their annual Sin City Shootout and literally had over two feet of dick between two point guards and a center.

Don't be intimidated by these group sports. And if you are, get stoned as fuck and go. I loved how dodgeballs would sting my face and help me feel alive every Tuesday in the West Hollywood Park, where I played with Team Amazeballs. Say cute stuff, like "Sweat is just fat crying," and if they laugh, you'll know they're an idiot and OK to fuck but not to date.

The easiest way to fool people into thinking you're in shape when you take your shirt off is to get some ab definition. The best workout for abs is easier than you know. It's actually walking. Just try walking away from the fridge at those commercials and instead get on the floor and do crunches. Your abs will not show unless your body fat is in proportion to your frame. Abs are basically made in the kitchen. Pilates is my favorite because almost every exercise relies on stabilizing your core. Throw down that dirty bath towel from your shower that morning and get to strengthening your trunk. I used to like jogging too, until someone posted a pic of me sprinting alongside a billboard that said SYPHILIS IS RUNNING RAMPANT IN WEST HOLLYWOOD and tagged me.

PERSONAL TRAINER TACTICS

It's a dog-eat-downward-dog world for personal trainers. Competition for clients is crazy. After working with go-go boys for a decade who all sun-lighted with PT work, I learned a few things:

■ Let word get out that you'll fuck your clients on the tenth session after purchasing a ten-session package. G'head and cross-fit your boss's slit.

■ Add a free five-minute rubdown at the end of the session.

■ Tell a client that you need some snapshots taken for a job you need to submit a picture for... 'cause you model and things. Chub up and let him do the dirty work.

How to **SUCK LESS** at

GYM GEAR

If I see someone wearing a Willam shirt to the gym, I know (a) they like nice things and (b) they probably swallow. What to wear while working on your fitness is sometimes a crapshoot. You wanna look cute, but you don't wanna look like you tried. You wanna stay streamlined, but you don't want it too tight. There's nothing wrong with wearing short shorts at the gym. It's all about what you wear with them that makes them offensive. Think athlete, not **asslete**. Thick thighs do

indeed make the dicks rise, but **brick** mugs only get hugs, so make sure you have a brow on at least if you're not a natural beauty.

Put in a little effort, but don't go overboard. This might be the only time I'd ever advocate brown eyeliner on anyone. Also, ladies, just so you know, leggings are not one size fits all. The "stretch" in stretch pants is not like a personal challenge for you. If you are wearing too small a size, they become sheer like a trampoline in the

This is Dick. See Dick in shorts. See Dick doing biceps and chest presses while also working his core.
Can you circle all the balls in the photo? Tweet me @willam and let me know.

sun...that nobody wants to jump on. Gentlemen, I would say the gym is the chance to wear what you would wear to cut the lawn—your dad's lawn, not yours. Try to keep both nipples covered. You don't need armholes down to your belly button. Jockstraps are great for the gym too, because boxers and briefs tend to give the wearer swamp ass rather quickly, and you know less is definitely more down there. Also, muscle shirts are for muscles. So sleeve it up if you've got sissy arms.

The gym is not the place to take pictures. We do not need to see your gains, bro. If you look good enough to be posting without your clothes, you're probably also hot enough to get laid and you should just delight in that instead of in look-how-hot-I-am posts about your leg day. If you really need everyone to see how good you look naked, make friends with people who have pools, Soho House memberships, or beachfront property. Pool parties are a great way to get in casual selfies. Make sure you take one of you in the outfit you arrive in and another in whatever you wear when you get wet so you double your picture ventures with regards to #tbt's and "missing the summer" winter posts as reminders to your friends that you are indeed a thirst monger.

SUCK LESS AT SOUNDS

WORKOUT EDITION

The perfect pump playlist is key for workouts. Adele songs in the gym are about as appropriate as the Black Eyed Peas at the dinner table. You need the perfect kinda jock jams with BPM that keep you moving. Here's sixty minutes worth.

"Faith" *George Michael*
"Ride for AIDS" *Alaska 5000 and me!!!!*
"LA Love (La La) [Jodie Harsh Remix]" *Fergie*
"Tambourine" *Eve*
"Say Yes" *Michelle Williams featuring (yes, featuring) Beyoncé and Kelly Rowland*
"Just Like Living in Paradise" *David Lee Roth*
"Gin in My System" *Big Freedia*
"Party in the USA" *Miley Cyrus*
"S&M" *Rihanna*
"Lifestyles of the Rich and Famous" *Good Charlotte*
"Back to the '80s" *Aqua*
"Three Small Words" *Josie and the Pussycats*
"Certified Freak" *Baby Bash featuring Baeza*

"I Seen Beyoncé at Burger King" *Cazwell featuring Jonny Makeup*
"Thick Thighs" *Willam featuring Latrice Royale*
"The Girl Is Mine" *99 Souls featuring Destiny's Child and Brandy*
"California Gurls" *Katy Perry*
"Talk Dirty" *Jason Derulo*
"Bye Baby" *Danity Kane*
"Countdown" *Beyoncé*
"Hella Good" *No Doubt*
"Gold Digger" *Kanye West*

For a cool down:
"Alien" *Britney*
"Reaper" *Sia*

How to **SUCK LESS** at
FOOD

17

- **BABY PEANUT BUTTER PACKS**—hard to get out and easy not to eat the whole tub. You can also dip a berry-flavored hair, skin, and nails vitamin in the peanut butter and get a great PB and J bite. I like the ones pictured.
- **HYDROXYCUT, ADDERALL, SUGAR-FREE ENERGY DRINKS** (I like Monster) and **5-HOUR ENERGY SHOTS**
- **BABY FOOD** should be thought of as healthy-people pudding. Sure, you could get some Acai Chia Raw Dessert, but that just sounds like a bowl of vegan yard waste. Lil' Bits by Gerber is delicious.
- **CHIA SEED PUDDING**—1 part chia seeds to 6 parts almond milk mixed with fruit or whatever
- **ALMOND MILK**—I buy one unsweetened chocolate one (zero grams of sugar per cup) and combine it with one presweetened (20 grams of sugar per cup). That way I get to drink it without it tasting like cocoa and cardboard and with half the sugar.
- **RICE CAKES** (brown)
- **SPINACH** in a salad or **EGG WHITE** omelet.
- **TURKEY BACON**—so good in the toaster oven. Everything is, in fact. Microwaves are the devil. Every morning as a kid I used to put

my forehead on the microwave door to watch while my eggs cooked, and look how I turned out.

- **JERKY**—high protein, low carb
- **TUNA**—high protein, low carb
- **SPOTTED DICK**—keep a can on hand in case you need an easy intro for a convo about STDs and protection. Put it by the bed if you've got a condition like herpes or HPV that isn't much of a threat when there's no outbreak present.

WILLAM

So your potential fuck buddy can see it and go "Spotted dick...?" and you can just say "Well, funny you should mention..." Bring it up. You'd wanna know if it was you, even if it's a 0.01 percent chance of exposure.

■ Some **FRUIT** you were gonna wash and eat but you'll probably just throw out once it starts to get mushy

■ **NUTS IN THE SHELL**—the opening of the shells makes it a good conversational snack and it's less grody than just shoving your dirty mitts into a honey-roasted peanut bowl. My husband used to have a jar full of unshelled pistachios or peanuts on hand for his basketball team buddies, including this one Black Irish dude, who I tried to offer another kinda social nut and then my husband got mad and put the nuts in the trash. (Hi, Patrick!)

If you're concerned about how quickly you get thickly, you may want to consider an eating disorder. One night I went to bed and realized I had had only soup that day. As I drifted off to sleep and/or passed out due to malnutrition, I was not only hungry but *proud*. Proud that I had recognized a problem I had, reclassified it as a condition, and used it as a tool to rationalize screwing up my body irreparably. Sure, my yo-yo dieting may lead to some minor organ problems down the road. But if I live to be, like, fifty-eight or fifty-nine instead of, like, in my seventies, it's fine by me. I'd rather be highly fuckable and get invited to the good parties than old and trying to learn how to work whatever remote control they have in 2064. WTF am I gonna do when I'm old other than be mad about how my diaper makes me look fat while looking at pictures of me young, saying "Shoulda had more sex." Nope. Not me. If I'm in a diaper it'll be from rectal prolapse due to dickdowns. This section will contain some medically unsound advice, but it's drag-queen tested and motherfucker approved.

Further caution: This section isn't for youths or cutter kids who just want to be loved or whatever. It's for grown-ass adults who are cool with hurting themselves a little to look cute on Instagram.

I struggle with bulimia. (Mostly spelling it. For some reason, my brain always wants to put two *l*'s in it.) I don't want you to think I'm just some advocate for unhealthy lifestyle choices. I totally am, but even more so, I'm a tireless warrior for beauty. So, yeah. That being said, let's talk about some ugly shit: vomiting. I'm not going to sit here and tell you which foods are hard to upchuck, because that would be irresponsible, especially if they were pizza, pies, or anything starchy or pointy, like tacos. Listing noodles, ice cream, and soup as easy ejections would also be equally horrendous of me. Most damning would be leaking that burp-inducing tonic water and soda bubbles make shoving stuff out the in door easier since burps are just little tiny baby voms…and that's why I won't say any of those sorta things.

Water is one of my first tips. I use water as a deterrent. Get in the pool or take a shower. If you eat in the shower or the bathtub, whether skinny or fat, you're a great big pig person. You're not a Pigpen, 'cause at least he had the good goddamn sense to eat his dirt in the yard. It's like how you bring a sandwich to the beach and you'll abandon it within three bites 'cause you're crunching on some sand. Same logic. So, yeah. First step: Get your ass in the tub to kill those munchies. And if you're OK with being one of those pig persons who eats dinner in the shower, go get a hamburger and check into the Beverly Hilton.

Once you're out of the water, find some reason not to sit down for the next hour, be it a self-tanner, Nair, or cellulite cream. Sitting down means in your head you'll probably be like "Oh, well, lemme get a nibble," and that is a call you do not need to answer. Take some fat burners or crack open a Red Bull. Remember, if you get dizzy or light-headed from not eating, that's Jesus telling you he likes you better thin (show me a fatty in the Bible). Now is a good time to paint your nails or give yourself a nice mani-pedi. The only thing more effective than the scent of nail polish remover as an appetite suppressant is homeless cock cheese.

I only grocery shop after eating a full meal and *never* stoned. Plan out what you'll be stuffing into your body, because if you shop hangry (hungry and angry), you're less likely to exercise control. Investing in a food scale for your kitchen is a great thing to do. Don't get the one off the floor and try to figure out how heavy your boneless, skinless cutlets are. That's nasty. I don't even own that kinda scale. When someone asks what I weigh, I usually just tell them, "One hundred and sexy, give or take a few loads."

When I go food shopping, I try to stick to the perimeter of the store. The middle is a buncha shit. All big calories with very few nutrients. Think about it—the left, right, and back are usually fresh produce, meats, and liquor. If you took

TRIGGERS

My favorite thing is maple anything. Consequently, I've recognized it as a trigger food and don't keep it in my house. But every year I get this autumnal feeling that a warm scarf and new pair of boots just won't satisfy. I'm talking pecan pie, pumpkin spice, and all that fall shit. Denying it does no good. I'll end up just sitting in an IHOP parking lot crying. So, I just grab a handful of maple pecans mixed with regular pecans and munch. They have them in bins at Whole Foods but if you eat them before you get to the front, they're free.

It makes sense. I'm a die-hard McGriddle maniac, so as an alternative to that, I make an egg white omelet with some maple sausage crumbled into it. It hits a maple note without the syrup-pocket-laden processed biscuit. I bought maple bacon one time, but the whole pack was gone within a weekend because I made pig candy in my oven like a fat ass. (Do not Google "pig candy" unless you have the willpower of a nun.) Jim Beam and Crown Royal both make maple whiskey too, and that tastes like a drunken pancake. I have that only once a year at Burning Man, and if

out of a supermarket all the foods that have added sugar, about 20 percent of the store would be left.

Eating the same amount of calories but eliminating refined sugars is the way to go. G'head and eat stuff with fat. Avocados, nuts, and butter (to a degree) are all cool. Due to a back injury, I had to stop working out completely in May of 2015. To compensate for that cardio dip, I changed my eat-whatever-I-want-and-work-out-six-times-a-week regime to eating Paleo foods with good fats and no sugar. I'm happy to report that as of June 2016, I'm the same weight. Granted, I was a bitch and a half on and off for about a month because of sugar withdrawals, but the desire to eat artificially sweet stuff waned. Getting rid of sugar resets your taste buds, if that makes sense.

This sounds drastic, but there are some little hacks to help you get back if cold turkey leaves you murky. There's this game called Chew and Spit that you do with your mouth where you chew up something and then spit it out. You only taste it while it's in your mouth, and that's what you're after, right? I see nothing wrong with it, especially if you do it near a garden. It's composting without the shit step.

If you absolutely cannot cut out alcohol, try a buttchug. It's far more dangerous, but you don't get all the pesky calories. (Look up a live performance of me doing "Only Anally" for a demo.) You can use any liquor you like, but don't do it with a Bloody Mary. It looks like a miscarriage.

there's any left by the end of the trip, I play "Here, Courtney, drink this" until it's gone.

See how I organized my eating disorder into a category that is less of a distinction of chaos and more just a preference? Like, I'm really anal about what I eat. Calling it "anal eating" isn't necessarily the best idea, but you get what I mean. When I'm craving caramel, I don't go out and get some Starbucks shit. I put a fuckin' Werther's Original in my mouth and have some almond milk. I've bought chocolate rice cakes as a substitute for eating a big piece of cake, and it works. You can even dip them in, like, vegan chocolate pudding from Whole Foods,

and if you smoke a fat enough blunt before, you'll forget that you outsmarted your thigh gap's demise via death-by-chocolate-chub.

Another great way to not binge is to light a candle. Not to pray for control but to get the flavor of whatever you want to eat. Since scent and taste are connected, lighting a good Yankee Candle in pumpkin spice alleviates my need to turn my mouth into a straight-up pie hole. If you want something tropical, light up a mango or coconut one because both those fruits are high in fat. You can also shove a vitamin C drop into a bottle of water and make a quick diet OJ.

Peanut butter pretzels with raspberries will give you that PB and J hit without as many carbs. You can also take some chili-powder coated mango and chew it up with some walnuts. Or dip those berry-flavored hair, skin, and nails vitamins in some honey almond butter like I said before. There. I just did a PB and J three-way for you with no bread at all.

How to SUCK LESS at MEAL PLANS

18

Now, before you get all big-booty Judy on me and toss this book aside to gorge, try drinking a cool glass of water. It'll fill you up and trick your brain into thinking your stomach is fuller than it is, because it literally is. You just filled it with water. Your brain is super stupid and real easy to fool, because if you're like me, you always know what the nice lady from *Scandal* is gonna do. Eating with a knife is a great tip too, and not just to cut your food. Try to eat ice cream with a knife instead of a spoon. You'll have to take small bites and be super careful and slow, picking out the little chunks of chocolate one by one. You definitely won't pig out, and with luck it'll melt by the time you realize *you shouldn't fucking be eating ice cream*. Dig out all the good chunks of cookie dough and be left with just a carton of raped and ravaged vanilla.

At this point I need to explain how I gained all this knowledge. I wasn't allowed to ride a pony when I was ten because the circus man said I would "hurt the horse." All my cousins and my sister got to ride the pony. I was fuckin' livid at that man, that pony, and the world. So I had a funnel cake. The next summer I was eleven and an elephant threw poop at me with his trunk. It was mating season at the San Diego Zoo and the pachyderms were pissed. I had to take my shit-encrusted shirt off and walk around topless, embarrassed by my teen tits, for a mortifying ten minutes before we found a gift shop to replace my shirt. I was a fat, fat, very fat kid who used food and humor and my very low threshold for what was morally sound to make me feel OK about being me (now I just stick to two outta three). My football trading card said I was 207 pounds and five foot three. The benefit of being basically a keg with legs was that for a good two years my coach made me the center and boys got to touch my ass while I passed a ball between my legs. They tried to switch me to the defensive line the next year and I would gobble a party pack of Bagel Bites each game-day morning to purposefully be over the weight limit for my age group. I also had ebola (a bowl of cereal, a bowl of pizza, and so on).

ABOVE: This is the face of tranvestite lactose intolerance. I ate six of these with three Lactaid pills and was fine. Pills for your ills.

So, yeah, I know pain. Social settings with food sometimes still scare the bejesus out of me. I'd rather have someone watch me shit than eat. Drugs can help with that by either making you not hungry or numbing your brain into acting normal. I like the latter because party food is usually so fun and each bite gets its own napkin. Some important things to remember when you're stoned around food is that you are not a pantry. You don't need all the food in you. It's never acceptable to tail a waiter at a party or event to see what he comes out with next. He'll think you're trying to blow him when you're actually just angling for a pig in a blanket… Oh, wait… Anyway…

I spent a lot of my youth in the South where unhealthy cooking is pretty much standard. Frying foods, putting cheese on everything and tons of carb-heavy dishes with pasta and breads are to blame for obesity, diabetes, heart disease and even incest (that last one because some people get too fat to leave the house and just touch on whatever's closest.) Limit your dairy. Remember, Mother Nature created cow's milk to help baby cows grow big and strong. Not to widen your rump roast.

…DOUCHE COMPLIANT

- Soups
- Poultry and fish
- Semen
- Chia seeds
- Popsicles
- Sushi (ask for "easy on the rice")

FLAVORITES OF WRONG

Broccoli.
Why would you wanna eat something that tastes *exactly* like what your farts are gonna smell like later?

Edible arrangements.
Never get 'em. Who wants to eat fruit after someone else has touched it? For all the same germs without the pesky vitamins, try just dating me or licking a truck-stop hooker's fingernails.

Chili.
Nah-uh. I don't fuck with no chili. No, sir. Chili is the sworn arch nemesis of bottoms the world over. Corn is Stalin to chili's Hitler (okra is like that bad guy from Korea). #Fuck-

fact: If you don't want to take my advice, at least employ the roll-with-it technique. Basically, you stick it in like normal, but under *no circumstances* should the penis be removed from where it's entrenched. Don't pull out; just carefully move stuff like you're playing Operation with a sex doll. Honestly, one position might be best if you want to avoid making the room stink.

Condiments.
They have a *lot* of sugar, which equals calories. Ketchup is made of tomato, which is a fruit and super sweet. Mustard and hot sauce are safe, but eighty-six those dressings, relishes, and anything with oil.

Anything at the movies.
My husband shovels popcorn so fast that at least a third of it ends up on the floor or his shirt. I'm like "Baby, slow down. You ain't even getting it all in your mouth." He's usually finished during the first part of the movie, then he ducks out to piss and comes back with a li'l something sweet, like some frozen ice cream mini bites or shit, while I just crunch my ice cubes and pretend they're organic Popsicle pieces.

Ramen.
If you eat prepackaged ramen, you don't love yourself. Why not just get in the tub and turn the water on real hot for an edible bath bomb? That way the noodles can touch all the parts of your body that'll be fatter once the ramen is ingested.

How to **SUCK LESS** at
HAVING THE MUNCHIES

Here are some pointers on how to eat stoned:

1. Make a list on what you're craving before you go stare into the void of the fridge.

2. There is no 2. This was a test.

Wait. I'm stoned and I forgot I had some ideas.

Just because you have no food in the house, that is no reason to resort to Postmates, Seamless, or Eat24. Many people see a take-out menu and instantly get a whole 'nother eating disorder. One where they're about to eat dis order of wings, dis order of fries, and dis here order of ravioli in a cream sauce even though they wanted it in a marinara (Fuck you, GrubHub). I think preparing your own meal somehow makes it more satisfying, and you're less likely to overspend because you're not playing Hungry Hungry Hippos in your head.

If you have a tendency to do a search-and-destroy mission for food while stoned, don't buy protein bars, because you will eat them like candy bars and rationalize that they're good for you. For protein, I like to use Grindr or just nibble hard-boiled egg whites. Split the cooked egg down the middle and spoon it out. Eat a little yolk from each half too if you don't mind the fat or egg farts. Whatever is kinda not cooked is my fave. Like yellow toe cheese. Fuck an omelet. No one has the time to wash a whole fuckin' pan, and you know it will just sit there 'cause it don't fit right in the dishwasher or you were gonna let it soak. My best friend used to say that to me. He was "letting it soak." Wash the fucking pan, faggot. Don't even look at a bag of Doritos either. Before you know it, you'll be holding the bag up to your mouth and doing that good ol' crumbdump move.

Actually, you can buy the Cool Ranch ones. The only thing I can imagine more refreshing than that signature Cool Ranch flavor is a dick that shoots Slurpee. But since God and 7-Eleven haven't debuted that kinda Big Gulp yet, here are more tips for satisfying the Cool Ranch craves.

Now, depending on how stoned you are, you may want to try these Willam-tested recipes, which offer that perfect umani bite to satisfy every craving box on your checklist. Some of them are just to keep you busy enough so you don't put your damn dirty finger directly into the jar of cookie butter like a pig. Just perfect little amuse-bouches combining all the flavors of home (Whole Foods, a dispensary, a Wawa, and a liquor store).

1 *Crush nachos.* **2** *Load Rubirosa.* **3** *Spread fat.*

LEVELS: BUZZED. STONED. CAN'T FIND YOUR FEET (CFYF).

1 French Food for Poor People. Snail on a teaspoon, lighter, salt, and pepper. Best enjoyed in a closed playground for that real crackhouse atmosphere. We wanted a picture of this, but the snail kept moving. They're transphobic, I think. **CFYF.**

2 Poor People's Margarita. Mountain Dew and Cuervo, and a funion rim. **BUZZED.**

3 I call this the Babysitter Special. PB, Benadryl, bacon bits, warm Hawaiian roll. It's a known fact that the ingredients in this sandwich are sometimes found on sets for dog food commercials to get that basket of puppies so docile. I model better on it, too. **STONED.**

4 Fruity Crackpebble Treats. Just like Rice Krispies Treats but better

because, well, drugs. Oh and use coconut oil to make your weed oil and it'll probably have some kinda vitamin B or some shit. **STONED.**

5 Eat all your weed candy and then fill the empty bag with cough syrup and grape soda for some Adult Capri Sun Fun. **BUZZED.**

6 1 minute grilled cheese. **BUZZED.**

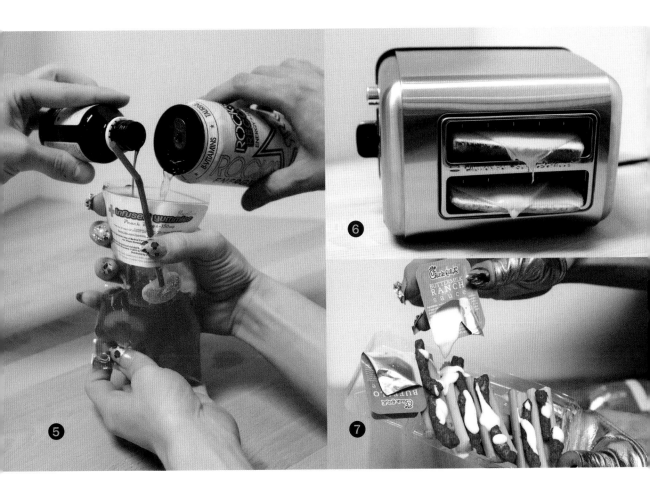

7 Get some celery and line up each stalk like those stupid Ants on a Log snacks they tried to make you eat at Bible camp. It kinda tastes like a vegan version of hot wings. **STONED.**

8 Ten-calorie Jell-O cups. 'Cause I mean even if you pig out and have four, it's still less than most other sweets. Plus, it's got protein (1 gram). Zero sugar. Zero carbs. And, yes, it does have chemicals, but when you die, they're probably gonna put formaldehyde in you, which is also a chemical, so really you're just kinda getting a head start. Better the chemicals now than having to buy a plus-size coffin later. Those are way more expensive. BUZZED.

9 Frozen nondairy creamers. For an ice cream shortcut, grab a couple of creamers from 7-Eleven in assorted flavors and chuck them into the freezer. Pop one open and squeeze it out. It's the perfect bite of custardy goodness for no fat and low calories. Use non-dairy ones if you're lactose intolerant. Thanks Dad for that one. BUZZED.

How to SUCK LESS at
SEX AND RELATIONSHIPS

've had sex with at least five hundred people. Starting a sentence that way might seem weird, because I'm going to end it saying I've also been in a super-committed relationship with my husband for almost fifteen years. I say "super committed" because I once tried to have him admitted on a 5150 due to fear he would harm himself or me. Love won, though. We have a crazy relationship, and it works for us. All six feet six inches of his Brooks Brothered self came into Micky's, where I told his tall ass that if he showed me his cock, he didn't have to pay cover. He whipped it out the way guys with giant dicks love to pull out their dicks any chance they can. I gave him a stamp and he went into the club. 'Bout thirty seconds later, he came back and said, "It's bigger now. You wanna see it again?"

That dick was so big I felt the need to start a new paragraph. It was the biggest dick I had ever seen on a white man. I immediately told my boss I was sick and we went to his hotel. We started dating after that and were pretty open about what we liked. He liked that I was "social." I mean he was able to pick me up straight outta my job within minutes of meeting me. I liked that he played

basketball and didn't feel the need to have some Ozzie and Harriet monogamy fantasy. He was traditional at times. Like, technically our first date was kinda dinner and a movie (I ate his dick while he filmed me on his 2002 flip phone). It's weird to say I'm still with my teenage boyfriend, but I am. We were engaged for literally three hours the morning we got married. I called him my Feyoncé 'cause "Crazy in Love" came on in the car on the way and that's what fags do.

Lesbians are the luckiest ever because there are so few variables. Example: I just went through my phone and found twenty-seven lesbian contacts. Out of those twenty-seven lesbians between the ages of twenty and however old my Aunt Nancy is, nineteen of them are in relationships (only four of them with each other too, so it's not stacked couples math there either). I have more than three hundred fags in my phone, and by the time I got to the *M*s, I had counted only fifty-two in relationships. It's a stereotype, but lesbians obviously have an urge to merge. Cohabitation is more likely to occur naturally with two women too, because women in general tend to settle down earlier in life and definitely

cheat less. So a relationship with two women is more likely to occur in the world than a lasting relationship with a woman and a man. Makes **furburgering** seem like the way to go, huh?

A man with a man is like a fuckin' dice game. I feel kinda bad for any hetero ladies who try to strap down a straight man, because it's a known fact that men cheat more. I don't need some geological Darwin chart to justify my dick gobbling. It's physically and biologically harder for men to be monogamous. Sure, we can, but damn. It's a bitch. Ladies, if a man cheats, it's because he

wants to. There are so many points along the way where you can avoid putting your dick into somewhere other than where you're supposed to. Bottom line. So either do better or just accept he's a dog. You can train a dog to act like a cat, but they'll always be a dog.

Based on that knowledge, my husband and I decided to not set ourselves up for failure by trying to pin each other down. We had fun together. We had fun apart. We were always (mostly) honest, though. And on the few occasions when we lied, we fessed up as soon as we were caught. He

ABOVE: See—he's not just a **husbank**. *He's cute, too.*

asked me what I did one weekend when he was gone, and before I could answer, he pointed to my elbows and knees and said, "Or should I say *who*?" because I had rug burn like a motherfucker from having sex on a carpet. He's a lawyer, so he always won arguments. (I also have a background in law—by that I mean I was arrested for battery.)

There may or may not have been times when one party would get wasted and completely cross over barricading the other party in the house. Now, I'm not saying who did what to whom, but keep in mind I was the kid who used to throw rocks at cars when they wouldn't stop to buy my lemonade. Learning that violence is never

I didn't get fucked by/fuck all five hundred guys, two girls, and three transpeople, but I've blown tons. I also didn't include instances where I blew a "str8" go-go boy while he watched straight porn on his phone to chub up for his next set because my publisher said we couldn't afford all that paper. There were also over three hundred or so three-ways, fourgies, fivesies, and straight-up sex parties to which I RSVPed my asstendance. Although, before you think my asshole needs a drawstring, at least a hundred to a hundred fifty or so of those multipartner encounters were with one specific guy who my husband and I kinda dated for a while as a throuple, so I'm not a total slore. Some three-ways should really only be counted as duos because there were a couple of instances during which the one guy was super hot so I slurped my way through his ugly BF just to get to him. We all been there, right?

And if you break it down math-wise, I'm barely even a slore at all. I figure each month for the past twenty years I've had one to five new sex partners. Some months more, some months none, but just to be safe, let's say two and a half partners. Two and a half partners per month times twelve months a year is thirty. If I'm thirty-four now and have been having sex since I was thirteen, that's five hundred lucky people. I've always practiced safe sex, to the point that I know I've only had five unprotected sex partners in my life. I had gonorrhea in my throat at thirteen, got crabs once when I was seventeen, and that's it for STDs. Safe sex works. I've had more loads dropped in me than a blind man at a laundromat, but I'm HIV neg, and that's because they've all worn rubbers. I wish I could give out free abortion coupons with the purchase of this book because I know the types of people who are my fans and I respect the struggle. I see you and I am you. Learn to swallow, honey. There are two kinds of ATMs in this world—one spits money and the other just spits, because nice girls don't swallow after going ass to mouth.

the answer will save you a lot of court time. All it took was getting my ass popped once the right way to learn that, and I thank my husband for it. "Spousal abuse" sounds so dramatic when really it was just two fags fighting, y'know? It's especially pertinent now not to smack nobody, because with gay marriage legal all over, if you hit your partner, it's called a "domestic disturbance," and they keep track of that shit. On the third house call to your home with DDs, somebody always gets hauled in, according to the one cop I used to pay to get rid of my parking tickets. In California, this is a result of O. J. Simpson. I consider myself lucky that I went to jail before Prop 8 got overturned because my basic battery charge gives me way more street cred. We got married 09/09/08 so our first anniversary would be 09/09/09, but then we ended up forgetting until the middle of September. Go gay marriage! We

were really hit or miss. Sometimes I wanted to hit him and sometimes I missed hitting him. It's all good now though.

While I got arrested for battery, I saw so many friends devoting their batteries to apps and dickstracted as fuck. I found a guy who is, like, 95 percent fitting into what I want. If there is a 100 percent match for me, that's nice, but I'm definitely cool with my guy. I'm not gonna try to spin the *Price Is Right* wheel to get one dollar even. I'm good with ninety-five cents. I've thought about chucking it all, but there's something to be said for not tossing in the towel. We've had our issues, but marriage is about making it work blah, blah, blah. I mean I actually like my job, so the idea that work can be both fun and rewarding isn't that foreign to me. Work can suck more balls than a Nerf gun though, too. If you're over it, try separating for a minute. Not necessarily to

SIDEBAR: ENTREPEWHORIAL ENDEAVORS

Some will read this section and say, "OMG Willam used to be a hooker at Dave & Busters." You're probably expecting a "but," so here you go. But.

In 2000, I was an androgynous seventeen-year-old working at a "gay gym" (read: bathhouse) each night from 7pm-3am after being fired from a dinner theater. After seeing all those dicks swinging for an 8 hour shift, I would usually try to get some action on the way home by making aggressive corndog-in-cheek motions at other drivers. After last call, I looked just enough like a girl for most men to not ask questions they didn't really want answered. This particular night, after getting the attention of a car with two men, we pulled up beside each other in an empty D&B parking lot. I ended up in the backseat with the driver while the other leaned on the hood and smoked/played lookout. Driverman busted in minutes and then handed me $50 telling me his friend was on deck. I was happy because John #2 was hot and I was hoping to blow him anyway. But now it was two birds, one big gay stone. Dollars AND dicks? Stop me if you see a drawback other than not knowing if my outcall rate was always gonna be buy-one-get-one for $50.

Being offered cash for sexual services was unexpected but did wonders for a former fat kid's self-esteem. I never thought anyone would think I was an actual Pretty Woman. Years later, a man (while literally inside me) looked me dead in the eyes and asked, "This is free, right?" and once again, I felt that surge inside me and then, again, a surge inside me.

Now here's the lesson: Receiving money for having sex doesn't make you a prostitute. ADVERTISING that you accept money for sex makes you a prostitute. Ho Long and Prosper.

MY FAVORITE ANSWERS TO INTRUSIVE RELATIONSHIP QUESTIONS

Q: Do you have an open relationship?

A: No just a capacity mandate from the Fire Marshall

Q: Don't you get jealous?

A: No but you would be if you saw my camera roll.

Q: How do you decide who does what?

A: I'm a human Chinese finger trap.

Q: Is this a permanent situation?

A: Not permanent. Just **spermanent**.

date new people but to try redating your person without all the rigors and stresses of why there are dishes in the sink when it was just as easy to put them in the fuckin' dishwasher. You might again find the reason you fell in love. You might find someone new. Going to bed mad won't kill a relationship, but waking up unhappy will. Each new day should yield so many possibilities, and feeling like you're stuck somewhere you don't wanna be is the pits.

So mix it up. Monopolies in business are never healthy, and it's kinda the same with a relationship. Having absolute power will eventually make one party feel shafted. The split can be 90/10, but that bit keeps each person in the gig happy with a stake in the success of it. If someone's 10 percent basically consists of looking good, being nice to their friends, and putting out, then there you go. Whatever works and keeps the seesaw swinging.

As you can now tell, I'm obviously qualified to help you with any relationshit problems. So keep reading, because you never know what kinda roadblock you might encounter in life. Whether a literal one or one near a campsite that you definitely didn't hear was cruisey in the Casual Encounters section.

SEX SOUNDS EDITION

Silent sex is no way to go. I'd definitely rather fuck a guy with an OK body and good musical taste than a gym bunny who tries to throw pipe to EDM. Put away the teddy bears and put on some Teddy and Backstreet and proceed to panty dropper land. Always have some good basics on the list, like Jodeci or Sade. Here's to not hearing anyone queef.

"All Day Sucker" *Stevie Wonder*

"West Coast (Lana Del Rey Remix)" *Travis Garland*

"Marvin's Room" *Drake (or the JoJo cover if you're a girl)*

"Pussycat" *Missy Elliott*

"Gorilla" *Bruno Mars*

"If" *Janet Jackson*

"Fire Meet Gasoline" *Sia*

"Freak-a-Leek" *Petey Pablo*

"Body Parts" *Courtney Act*

"Love Yourself" *Justin Bieber*

"Life in the Fast Lane" *Eagles*

"Pink" *Aerosmith*

"Free" *Graffiti6*

"How to Love" *Lil Wayne*

"Rock the Boat" *Aaliyah (Great for blow jobs! Bounce the bed to make them move a bit.)*

"5 O'Clock" *T-Pain featuring Wiz Khalifa and Lily Allen*

"Black and Gold"—*Sam Sparro*

"One Word" *Kelly Osbourne*

"Superpower" *Beyoncé featuring Frank Ocean (The beat throbs and so should you.)*

"I Don't Mind" *Usher*

"Demonstrate" *JoJo*

VIRGINS

Hey, virgins. *If you're reading this with a V card, that's cool. Take your time. When you find the right person, make sure all signals are go before you try to get frisky. See if she's maybe a little wet or if he's hard. Don't be scared of taking off your clothes. If they're in bed with you, they probably like the way you look, so at least be confident that you're doing good so far. You're probably gonna get laid. Nobody's body is exactly how they want it. Y'know when you see a burger and the bun don't fit it? You still wanna eat it, right? Hell yeah. If you know you ain't got the dick of death swinging down there, make sure you satisfy them some other way. If you're at a point when you're in your drawers and no one is running away yet, cool. You can fuck me with a fiver, but you better be doing it like you got eight and a half inches. Chances are if you do it right, I'll ask what your real name is to save it in my phone. And hey, if it ends with you just **disasturbating** and crying, that's weird but OK, too. If stuff doesn't look like it's gonna work within five minutes or so, best to call a rain delay on the game. 'Cause, I mean, if you can't be good, the least you can do is be quick.*

If for any reason you aren't into it, just stop as opposed to sucking through the abyss of it all. Acting like a lazy, kinda-into-it, kinda-not Eeyore in bed will get you donkey punched or really make your partner call into question his skills. Sex shouldn't be silent. Talk. Make jokes. Tell each other what you want and what you like. Act like the people on the sites that you can't access on public Wi-Fi. A good blow job should be noisy. It should sound like a Dyson underwater eating an octopus. Make sure you have some background noise, too. One of my favorite amateur videos kinda sucks because I can hear South Park in the background. There's one twerking video I used to watch of this big-assed dude that I always had to mute because Kelly Rowland is screeching over it. That's why I recommend the "Sex Sounds Edition" playlist if you're gonna fuck around champagne-room style.

LAP DANCE TIP

Pick a mid-tempo song from whenever the lap dancee was going through puberty.* I always imagined what a lap dance to "Bye Bye Bye" by NSYNC would be like, 'cause I just think of all the bouncing and package grabbing. If you're slick and you got the moves, anything can fly.

"No Diggity" Blackstreet
"Baby One More Time" Bowling for Soup
"Ride" Ciara
"Rack City" Tyga
"Boyfriend" Justin Bieber
"Closer"—Nine Inch Nails
"I Just Wanna Love You" Jay-Z
"Rich Girl" Hall and Oates
"My Pony" Daniel Wesley
"The Wire" Haim
"Cream" Prince (but only if they're gonna nut)
"My Favorite Mistake" Sheryl Crow (The opening guitar lick alone…)

Obviously, I'm not saying pick Kidz Bop songs. If anyone sees this as me schooling pedophiles, please know that's not the T. I'm not encouraging minors to have sex with adults either even though I did *a lot*. Adults having sex with underage people is never gonna stop as long as there are horny teens who lie. Some don't even have to because parents and the law do very little to govern it as long as no one is crying foul. (Hi, Kylie Jenner and Tyga.) Did my having sex with a buncha grown dudes hurt anyone? No. I have a great father, so it wasn't daddy issues and I was emancipated and on my own by the time I was sixteen. I was going down on this one DILF in a waterpark bathroom once near closing time, and we heard a voice all of a sudden go "*Dad*?" and this dude grabs my head like he's in a balloon-popping contest. It was obviously his kid. We stood soooo still for like fifteen seconds, dick just straight-up in my mouth like a slowly deflating water balloon. I laughed then and I'll laugh now. I was fifteen at that point, so it's not that bad. I'm writing about this not to brag about being a teen porker poking bag but more to warn all the people reading this who one day might have a gay kid or, hell, any kid. Get them Gardasil vaccines and don't be ashamed to talk about sex. My mother told me about oral sex when I asked why a blow job from a vampire would be bad. (Coincidentally, I was Vampira the next year for Halloween.)

Everybody is probably gonna learn what cum tastes like at some point in their lives, and it hopefully won't taste like green freezer pops and bleach. If you're reading this and you're underage, and you're thinking, "Wow, how did Willam get so

---

* Disclaimer: If you are an underage virgin, please skip this part (or go read it in your yard). If you are an eighteen or older virgin, please let any one of your four cats sit on this book.

much play as a kid?" it was kinda word of mouth (ya get it?). Some boys on the football team mentioned me to some ROTC guys, and pretty soon it was on. It probably helped that I was first-chair saxophone, and anyone who plays a woodwind instrument knows how to give bomb-ass head. Mostly because you have to learn to wrap your lips around the mouthpiece so your teeth don't touch it. Marching band was basically blow-job

boot camp. I was obese and not that cute until I was about fifteen, so there are those who will argue that every time I slept with someone, it was basically them telling me, through semen deposits, that I was attractive, was not too fat to function, and/or didn't smell like *queso*. Having gonorrhea at thirteen didn't slow me down either. I mean, sure, my parents were surprised to find out it wasn't strep throat, but it technically wasn't

WHEN YOU THINK YOU GOT AN STD/STI

- When it burns during your morning piss after you've had sex but it's actually just your piss hole glued shut with dried semen. Gotta let that hot, salty pee burst right forth through it like a Brave Little Toaster. If your subsequent streams sting, get checked.
- When you're low-key looking for ingrowns in your happy trail or blackheads to pop on your arms and you see a freckle relocate. That mole ain't moving. That's crabs—so still technically not an STD/STI but nasty just the same.
- When you shit blood. Sometimes you just got ripped open while fucking. Slow down on your shit chute, Mary, and warm it up before you go trying to pull a cable car's worth of dick into your bay area. Throw a few soapy fingers up there in the shower until

your hole is stretchier than Mr. Fantastic.
- When your piss turns weird colors. Maybe you got punched in the kidneys and you're just pissing some blood (reddish) or you took too many uppers (bright yellow) or you got stoned and ate a buncha Flintstones kids' chewables because it was the only thing in the house other than ketchup and soy milk (brown).
- When you have a cold sore on your face. I know full well that I wasn't licking stick before I knew my times tables, and yet I've been getting cold sores since I was a kid.
- Rash gash, aka razor burn, aka chub rub. Chub rub is usually centrally located between the thigh and genitals in areas that rub together due to them being big enough that they rub together.

my fault since at thirteen, even though I was the aggressor, I was statutorily raped (and they say you can't rape the ~~willing~~ Willam). Still, my parents knew it was my own fault and made me talk about safe sex with some gay dude my mom worked with at the hospital, so at least they were covering their asses. I ended up fucking around with him nine years later when I went home for the holidays. There are only so many things you can do on Christmas break before you start fucking your parents' friends, right? (Hi, Craig! Thanks for making that joke to my father about me calling you "Daddy," too. Precious memories.)

PS: Don't ever try to fuck in socks. They kill your traction if you're fucking on wood or tile, and no one wants your sock next to their face.

BIRTH CONTROL AND PROPHYLACTICAL THINGS

Helen of Troy was one of the great icons of beauty. Story goes she was the face that launched a thousand ships and the cause of the Trojan War. I'm pretty enough that I too find myself embattled in a Trojan war almost nightly. By that, I mean I have to fight with dudes to put on a fuckin' Trojan. They always try "It doesn't fit" or "I can't feel anything." At times like this you gotta value that beauty you have. 'Cause if you get some STD, certain parts of you won't feel so attractive. No one has ever said "Wow, those scabs really add to the landscape of your genitals" or "Damn, that facial wasting looks good on you." Value your body and how it looks, and if someone won't respect your wishes when they want to enter your temple, well, then it's time to look further into the congregation and find someone else to worship you, goddammit. I'm not saying I'm a face that can launch a thousand ships, but I for sure fucked around behind a dock with some Jet Skis in Whorelando.

I know someone who doesn't want to have kids because she's got an alcohol issue. It's not that she's an alcoholic. It's just that she thinks the kid will steal her vodka. Morons like this make me realize there are too many assholes and mouths relying on the planet and not doing anything in turn for it. It's really starting to hurt this big watery rock we're living on. So birth control and the occasional "selective reduction" are great.

How to **SUCK LESS** at
TRUST

"**T**rust is a gift," my marriage counselor told me. I coulda gotten that from a needlepoint pillow without a co-pay, so my husband and I only went to her once. You don't want to know everything about whoever you're in a relationship with. It's like watching a movie and knowing the ending. A little bit of mystery is always good. My husband and I had a phone rule: We could look at each other's shit whenever we needed to. He would regularly text for me on my phone when I drove, and vice versa, so there was no hiding things. My photos were all 3-D: dick, drag, or my dog. We were open and it worked really, really well.

Except when it didn't. As I said, he's a lawyer so he thinks he can lie really well, but I'm an actor and I lie, like, professionally. That's all that acting is: lying really well. When he lied, it turned into Tony Danza doing Shakespeare: lotsa stuttering and trying to get outta it. If someone says they didn't do coke but then your tongue is numb after making out with them, trying to lie is useless. Best to fess up immediately. I don't need the reasoning when I had already tasted the seasonings. We were also both slobs about cheating. He would find the tiniest sliver of gold on the floor and bust me for my Magnum litter. Having my yellow lab

throw up a condom on a Monday after he was gone was also probably not the best way to interrupt dinner. Finding a pillow on the floor after I was gone for a weekend right where he liked to get blow jobs was kinda tough to explain. In both cases it wasn't cheating, because we were open. It was "Oooh yeah, I was gonna tell you…"

People cheat for the sole reason of getting something they're not getting in their current circumstances (i.e. particular sex acts, thrill of the anonymous new partner or self destruction). Plain and simple. I had my husband's dick in my hand within thirty seconds of meeting him, so for him to expect me to go from ho to housewife would've been ridiculous. Also, there's the little fact that I run a stripper agency. Am I supposed to just look at the dicks? I mean really? Blow jobs are how strippers say "Sorry for being late" or "Will you count my ones for me?" It's when the extracurriculars become more of an entrée than a side dish. That's when you gotta worry. If you find out you're being cheated on, make a game plan before you do anything crazy. Try to figure out what made them want to cheat. Do you suck in bed or are they just tired of the same ol' same ol'? This could be a learning experience on how to improve your chances of getting someone to

SLY TIPS FOR GETTING THE TIP ON THE SIDE

- *Make sure you put sexcessories back in the exact same spot.*

- *Keep the condom count consistent.*

- *Wipe doorknobs, faucets, and light switches anyone may have touched.*

- *If you're a mobile ho on the go, hide all your shit under a fake symbol. Like any pics of me playing Cheater Cheater Penis Eater are hidden with the Private Photo Vault app. Any hookup tools are under utilities because I like that it sounds like "You little tease," which I'm not. Teases don't put out. A favorite trick for saving numbers and pics you shouldn't be saving is to name them as a food place that matches their ethnicity. So that hot guy named Tony who smoked you out and went down on you is now Uncle Tony's Italian Bakery…'cause he got you baked, right? Little fun things to remind you what a skank you are. Just make sure the sushi place doesn't text you, reminding you to stop for lube on the way over. Tell tricks it's a work phone and not to text you under any circumstances because you leave it at work sometimes to download software. G'head and lie, but know that karma can give the worst kinda reach around.*

remain faithful. If you're just done and don't care, I recommend destroying their ass so bad that they have to reset their whole life to factory settings. Fuck them one last time and "fall back" while reverse cowgirling/boying. Snap that shit. It heals in like six weeks. If it's a woman who's creeping on you, be more careful, because they press charges and have dads. Try a simple thing like a few dead gerbils scattered about before you give back her key. Rats work too, but gerbils show intent better.

Pour one out for 'em and move on...

How to **SUCK LESS** at
BREAKUPS

My dude bought a pair of Crocs for himself for Christmas in 2014. I considered it abusive behavior. We separated in February 2015. Anyone who ever thinks it's OK to not care about their appearance so much that they deem it acceptable to wear something that ugly deserves to be alone. So I left him for a full year. We reconciled when I realized I'd rather be 95 percent happy with him than exhaust myself searching for the 100 percent I probably would not find. I figured if it came to a point when we wanted to get back together, we would. Our separation was actually pretty chill.

Things hadn't been going well and we both knew it. Sometimes it takes a big gesture. I hired really, really hot guys from Real Rock 'n' Roll Movers, who took their shirts off to get my shit outta our shared house. I still slept there for about a month because just the threat of me moving out wasn't enough. It took the big gesture. I woke him up one morning looking cute. Human hair lace fronts out the door, sunglasses on, NutriBullet in my hand with the cord wound up all around it, and I told him, "Car's on the way. Leaving on a jet plane." I was actually just moving to Inglewood, which pissed him off even more because he knew he was the only white guy I'd ever dated. He

didn't even try to argue. I know he felt defeated. He probably just envisioned me rebounding like a trampoline with some guys around me yelling, "Now make that muthafucker bounce."

Sadly, that big moving-out gesture still wasn't enough. Sometimes you need one good last fight to throw some shit or cry—one or the other, not both. Then ya gotta walk away. I didn't talk to my husband for six weeks straight when I left him. Total ice. Remember in the Gold Bar when I let Phi Phi scream at me and I just sat there composed? Same idea. Give them nothing to work with. No response for him was even worse than all the back and forth because we couldn't continue the same vicious cycle we'd gotten ourselves into. I thankfully had a mutual friend to help with my shared dog custody and financial entanglements with him, but exes will still try to climb over that wall. If it's finally time to get back together, another milestone should be offered up. A ring, a getaway, or a gesture, like your partner finally bottoming for you after not doing it for the past decade.

Not that I wanted him to bottom. We had both gained weight while we were together and that was an issue for us. He worked a lot harder than I did, leaving him less time to focus on his body. Being a Midwest boy, his food choices steered toward the heavier meat and potatoes too, so that didn't help. It was really difficult for me to address it, and I would only think of it as I saw his utensil go to his mouth. It's like Romy not letting Michele eat that one Dorito she had in her hand before they started their diet.

But, truth be told, if someone gains more than ten or fifteen pounds and it shows, you're allowed to bring it up. That's like bringing a third person into the relationship, 'cause that's how much, like, a real fat baby could weigh. If anyone argues otherwise, tell them a drag queen justi-

fied it with math. I tried sitting my guy down and telling him I was into hot daddies, and by that I meant in-shape older guys with their shit together, not guys who looked like they were pregnant with their second child.

If the marriage is just not working, there's usually some straw that breaks the camel's back. I once told a girl to cut her bangs, and I really believe that gave her the courage to leave her marriage. (Hi, Seana!) I also informed her afterward about her husband sending me dick pics and that I supplied the piñata for his bachelor party after they were separated, and that was probably TMI

SUCK LESS AI SOUNDS

SULKING EDITION

Please don't cue up Tammy Wynette as soon as you break up with someone. That is a horizontal slash across the wrist, and the songs in this playlist are three vertical slices that'll get the job done better.

"Ring Off" *Beyoncé*

"Picture" *Kid Rock featuring Sheryl Crow*

"What About" *Janet Jackson*

"Another Lonely Night" and "Ghost Town" *Adam Lambert*

"What's Going On" *Remy Ma*

"All I Wanna Do Is Make Love to You" *Heart*

"When Love Hurts" *JoJo*

"Love Lockdown" *Kanye West*

"Should've Been Us" *Tori Kelly*

"You're So Vain" *Carly Simon*

"Just a Fool" *Christina Aguilera featuring Blake Shelton*

"Save Up All Your Tears" *Cher*

"Mirrors" *Justin Timberlake*

"99 Problems (But a Bitch Ain't One)" *Jay-Z*

"Go Your Own Way" *Fleetwood Mac*

"Into the Blue" *Kylie Minogue (This one was my play-every-day jam.)*

"Hotel California" *Eagles*

"This War" and/or "Blood from a Stone" *Shoshana Bean*

"Blank Space" *Taylor Swift*

"Sister Christian" *Night Ranger*

"Goodbye Earl" *Dixie Chicks*

"Just Give Me a Reason" *Pink featuring Nate Ruess*

"I Hate Myself for Loving You" *Joan Jett and the Blackhearts*

"How Come U Don't Call Me Anymore" *Prince*

for her. By "provided the piñata," I mean he tried to bust me open with a stick once. I was so happy when she left his ass, but she did miss him. I had some cut-and-paste Internet meme on my phone 'cause my sister had just been flat left, so I forwarded it to her, but I still remember it. It was something like "It's hard when you miss people. If you miss them, it means you were lucky. It means you had someone special in your life who's worth missing." Bullshit, right?

We all cope in different ways after a breakup. I like sex and being awesome. I think more people should try it instead of limping back to an ex for casual sex. Waiting at least a year for that shit helps remind someone why they moved on, even if the dick was right. The month and a half without speaking to my temporary ex after I left him was really rough on him. But that straight-up Elsa meets Casper frozen 'n' ghosting is the way to go. After someone shows you who they are and you then try to change them to your liking, and it fails miserably, it's best just to cut the cord and leave. If you don't, you better have a better game plan than sex as a weapon or fucking up their car, because I've tried both and they only offered momentary relief, like a topical ointment. You can also just watch *The Color Purple* with a blunt and learn about what real pain is.

WILLAM'S FAVORITE STRIP CLUBS

Strip clubs are a great way to distract yourself after a breakup with penises, titties, and four-dollar ATM fees.

Atlanta, GA—Swinging Richards. *I've made MANY poor financial decisions here. Five stars.*

East St. Louis, IL—Boxers 'n Briefs. *Dirty couches but it's not like you came for the upholstery… where someone else may have actually come.*

Fort Lauderdale/Miami, FL—Le Boy *for twinks/twunks;* Boardwalk *for muscle; back room of* Twist *is muy caliente latino hunks.*

Las Vegas, NV—Spearmint Rhino. *A few* Rock of Love *girls work there still.*

NYC/SoCal—The Adonis parties. *So much penis.*

San Francisco, CA—Nob Hill Theatre. *("Theatre" is spelled fancy so be couth. Don't nut on the floor.)*

Washington, DC—Secrets. *Guys so dirty they installed a shower for you to watch them get wet in.*

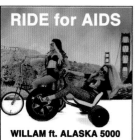

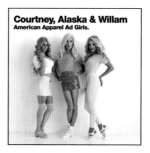

How to **SUCK LESS** at

DIGITAL DATING

23

ating profiles should always leave whoever's viewing it wanting something: wanting to see more, wanting to find out more, wanting to find out if they really aren't here to hook up. Brevity is the soul of wit. That means keep it short and funny. If you're bad at jokes, put the beginning of a knock-knock joke in and see if anyone says "Who's there?" When strippers would take photos for picture-submission jobs I was casting, I would tell them to keep two things in mind: look friendly and look desirable. Nobody wants to see a professional Blue Steel glare from a magazine editorial you did. A quick glance should net any viewer two and a half outta the following three things: intelligence, stability, looks. I know it seems like a lot to convey in a short profile, but think of it this way: When you eliminate the negative, more positives have room to show. Don't put "Looking for a new workout buddy," because then it looks like you're not motivated enough on your own and may be out of shape. Writing "Looking for a roommate" is dead wrong, too. I don't want you eyeballing my dresser when you're fucking me, wondering if there's room for your socks. No, sir...and you can't use my building's gym on the way out. This is a doorman building. Punch it and roll out. I want my parking pass back, too.

Nothing makes me want to write back less than a clothed headless torso as a profile pic, especially if it's a site geared toward more than just hooking up. You can always reply to these mystery-man queries with "Looks like you forgot to fill in your stats and put up a pic." I mean c'mon. Make me ask one fewer question. A face should be a given. If someone sends you a torso shot, give their headless horseman ass directions to Sleepy Hollow. Go fuck up Ichabod Crane's world. *Bye*. Having a pic with your face visible and a toned body (or your shirt off if you're a guy) provides so much intel for someone deciding whether to further explore options with you or just hit BLOCK. Showing that you're confident with your body is such an earmark of authenticity. I'm sure you have a great personality, but personalities don't make dicks hard and pussies slick, do they? You need to get them into the store with the window display and then sell them with the product's features. I've found that if someone doesn't have a shirtless shot but will send three dick pics, chances are he's still gonna tell you he's in shape. Unfortch for you, that shape is a bloated polygon. Like, you can take pics of your junk but can't show me that the only spare tire you got is in your trunk? *Bye*.

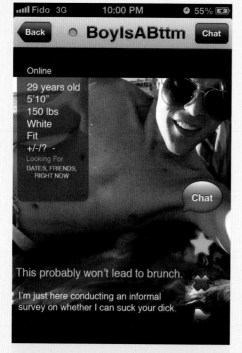

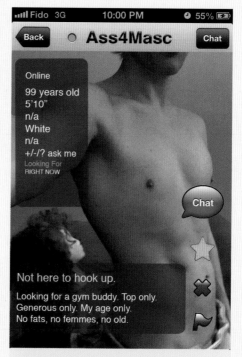

This would constitute a good profile. And I say that because this is what I've been using since I took the pic in Hawaii last year. It gets me laid. If you look closely enough, I'm laying on a towel with my own picture on it so it's not like I'm trying to hide that I crossdress for money and attention in between dick buffets.

This is just bad. Remember to consider your background when selecting profile pics. I mean, a wig in the background could mean the guy is a hairdresser. But that begs the question, does he do color or just cuts? And if so, does he sell coke like that one guy at Shorty's? Additionally, not being forthcoming with pertinent details and contradicting information would lead to me hitting block.

YOU CAN CALL IT "E-FUCKERY"

Guys, you have to ask nowadays if the person you're talking to has a penis. It's like how sometimes sandwiches at the airport don't list tomato as an ingredient but then, lo and behold, you unwrap it and there it is. Some of these girls' surgeons are real fuckin' slick. Just make sure.

Masc Vers Power top on Prep for Masc vers power btm on prep. Blond only (no ash bases). 24 hour on weekdays. Golds on weekends.

BarebackRT *A social networking site for drag queens. Just kidding. It's short for Bareback Real Time.*

Adam4Adam *For people still with AOL addresses, masseuses, and party play. Lots of guys who want to meet in cars or on nature trails after park hours.*

Tinder *For people who might want to date each other after they do the I-never-do-this-kinda-thing things on the first date.*

Grindr *For powder people, be it protein, cocaine, or the bronzer they dust up with.*

Scruff *The San Francisco to LA's Grindr. More hair in more places.*

Blendr *Straight people Grindr but with lots of* **trahnz,** *too.*

GROWLr *Oink, woof, snort. Animal noises rule here because you're supposed to let anyone sniff your ass or else you're shallow or a body elitist.*

Craigslist *CL people tend to want to keep things on the low—their activities, their standards, and the graves they've possibly pre-dug for your freshly fucked corpse.*

Ashley Madison *For blackmailers and people who weren't raised right. Check it out. It's super fun.*

ItsJustLunch *For people too busy to find their own tail but who will eat a salad instead of just diving into the business-lady special between the legs.*

POF *"Plenty of fish" pretty much stands for "plenty of fuck" 'cause everybody wanna smash.*

Eros *Another social networking site for individuals with mix-and-match genitalia, money on their minds, and a timer on their phones.*

Backpage *Like the back page of a dirty local magazine.*

Jack'd *A great spot to find urban ass and more DL than D. L. Hughley.*

119

Specificity is key. You don't have to fill in everything. Like, if you don't have a pet, leave it blank. Don't write "Doggy in the corner with door unlocked." Say what you're looking for instead of what you are. Put out into the world what you want to attract and it's more likely to come to you. I just wrote that because it sounds true, but I have no clue if it is.

I do know you should never say "Looking for tops," because that makes you seem like a greedy whore bottom. Say you're looking for a top. Singular. I mean you only have one asshole, so unless it's Pride or someone's anniversary, one should suffice. Or wait. I forgot about three-ways. Then you could say "tops" plural. But if it's a weekday, you'll look like a skank. Weekdays are for finding new people to fuck. Weekends are for fucking the good ones again.

One great icebreaker to talk about is safety. Ask them how they scored on their last HIV test. Did they win? I'm a big safety girl, so I always have a spare OraQuick rapid-result test on hand. Remember that episode of *SaTC* where homeboy said to Samantha that he couldn't fuck her or eat her the way he wanted to until she got an HIV test? Well, this test is great because you can do the quick swab test and just fool around and get handsy for fifteen to twenty minutes while the results develop. Then you can decide if the tasting menu will include a pig in a blanket or just straight-up wiener.

Anyone who leaves a status or preference blank kinda makes me wary. Like, don't make me ask. It's there for a reason. Some guys prefer to hook up only

with sereo-coordinate guys. Some take twenty loads on a Tuesday. Let people know what they're in for. I got to a guy's house once and found out he was in a wheelchair. I saw a giant dick on the profile and hopped right in the car, didn't think to ask about basic motor functions. Not that I minded. Riding dick is a fave, and his upper body was so jacked from all the rolling he did. Everything was right as rain and I woulda run a telethon for his ass by the end of the night. But again: Ask questions. Say "Hey, anything I should know? Crazy neighbors, no furniture, missing limbs, handicapped ramps?" Wheelchair dude ended up not calling me back after I wanted to hang out again. I really liked him, but I'd rather keep my pride than chase anyone who isn't into me, especially 'cause he probably had some sorta motorized scooter that could outlast my wind power.

If someone doesn't make a move after you present the option, then bounce. Put the coin on the dresser and hit the door. Sex is just sex sometimes. Maybe you were OK for a taste but not a swallow. Whatever. You're gonna strike out sometimes. As a rule, I hit on everyone to a degree and eventually someone says yes. Y'know, like you make a joke that may or may not be you hitting on them. Like after swimming, say "Wow, dick. I didn't know there'd be all that dick. Let's snorkel." Obviously, their penis wouldn't be a suitable device for underwater air delivery, but if they ain't into you, they'll overlook it. It's cool.

I tried and failed to get with a lot of my friends. Had I persisted and tried to shove their genitals into my mouth, I may not have the buddies I have today. Like when I'm trying to not eat a ton, I always remind myself that there will be other meals. Use the same principle. Don't talk to me about YOLO either. It's just a douchebag way of saying seize the day, and you should never seize someone's genitals. There's no castle between your thighs where Wario has hidden the princess and Yoshi. I repeat: YOLO doesn't apply to genitals. If a friend says *no*, let it go.

Now that we're on a genitalia-based topic, let's go back to pictures. Block anyone who leads with a butthole pic. I think your profile pic should be you in whatever amount of clothing you'd be comfortable in when answering the door. I'd answer in boxers, so I'll put up one in boxers. It's gotta feel unforced. Balancing the effortless appearance of a profile with how much actual work went into it can be deceiving. Maybe proofread it with an honest friend. The goal is to get

dick and not to sound like a dick while correcting other profiles' grammatical errors. If you can't get a simple homonym right, I'll probably wonder if you'll be able to figure out how the intercom works to ring me when you're at the gate. Education is important, but big biceps are importanter. Again, no one's ever asked for a picture of a diploma on Tinder.

Those who say they can't send out a picture that's easily identifiable are probably fakes. Even worse are those who won't give an exact address (it happens!). Vague "Meet me on the corner of" doesn't play well with me. A desire to keep one's creep game on the low is fine, but don't ask someone to follow some *Goonies*-like adventure just to get into your place—telling them to park, then wait for a guy with a dog, but if you see the gate open, come through, but take your shoes off and then come in through a window. I wanna fuck, not play Mouse Trap.

HOW NOT TO GET HUSTLED

(FULL DISCLOSURE: I was one of the people in the following story and I won't say which one.)

Once upon a time, Man #1 was looking for some fun so he decided to get some head from Man #2 who he had just met on the internets. Man #2 walked up in Man #1's hotel room and immediately put on some music. They ended up by the bed and #2 started to make balloon animals with the #1 standing up. #1 eventually sat down and #2 slid up #1's body and grabbed some pillows. One for his knees and one for behind #1's head. #1 laid back and relaxed while #2 quietly went through the pants of #1's which were around his ankles still. Once in that wallet, #2 took all the money and put the wallet back in the pocket from whence it came. Then the other dude came. They all lived **fucktardely** ever after.

Draw what I'm runing from.

How to **SUCK LESS** at
REBOUNDING

Fuck buddies are perfect for right after a breakup. Not everyone you fuck is gonna turn into a relationship. I know people who have fucked me, then seen me the very next day and wouldn't have pissed on me if I were in a dumpster fire (that was a nickname I had once, BTW). Fucking someone multiple times and hoping their NSA attitude will change is also a bad idea. Hamsters don't turn into unicorns. If someone tells you or shows you who they are, believe them. I know that many people think sex activity occurring multiple times over many months can kinda shift things, but fuck buddies sometimes never turn into anything more. Sex is fun, and people like to have fun with their friends. There's nothing wrong with enjoying someone else's physical company and then not wanting to have to ever put on a suit around them or meet them for sushi. I literally just wrote this section on a plane coming home from the UK, traveling with a really good friend I casually fucked. I'm not allowed to say his name because it would make all our mutual friends go "Ewwww," so maybe keeping the social and the sexual further apart than what would be normal isn't a terrible idea.

Now, everybody wants what they can't have, right? You ever think about hitting up your friend's ex? I sure have. Here's the math to figure out whether it's OK to do so: You need to wait one week for every month they were together before you can fuck them. If you want to blow them, you have to wait three to six weeks, depending on how many people live in your town. Also, get real schwasted so you can at least blame the alcohol. If you see somebody who is basically yours even though you ain't together at that exact moment, there are a few things to do: (a) make sure he notices you somehow; (b) remove any jewelry and get a hair tie just in case some shit goes down; (c) be a fuckin' adult and go about your day; or (d) all the above. Please remember that dick is an organically recurring natural resource. Every time a male baby is born, more dick gets released into the wild, so there is never a dick drought. Be prepared to get friend fired if you get caught. Also, if you do go through with it, make sure your friend whose ex you're fucking with doesn't have "Share my location" on your texts with you and others.

HOW TO GET A TRICK

Hooking up is like beer pong. Everyone should have fun, and way to go if it leads to a championship round or an actual relationship. But you can't let championship stakes affect how you do in the first round. Knowing the diff between the kinda date whose armpit you lick and the kinda date whose armpit you cuddle up in is imperative. The kinda person you would give the last Totino's pizza roll to. Sometimes it's just not a comfortable thing. There's one guy I ever actually cuddled with and I only did that because I was afraid that if I made him pull out, I was gonna shit on him but it was all good and he ended up giving me his dog tags. I made him feel good, so he gave me jewelry. It's all about value. You want someone who values your time and skills while appreciating that some fun won't fuck up their current day-to-day life.

Many men will act all cuddle buddy on the low but turn into rapists on the go once their dick blood gets going. The casual spoon will turn into a forcible fork real damn quick. They act all surprised by their boner and said "Sorry" literally seconds before trying to shove it in. It's like trying to blow a bubble after two chews on a new stick of gum. No. Same goes for you bottoms. If he gets a little hard, that's cool. It's a compliment. But don't take that as an all-systems-go sign and try to shove all that barely half-masted dick up your ass. Suck it first. "Lick it before you stick it" was definitely not something Moses said, but it's a goddamn commandment to me.

If I'm trying to turn a friend into something more, I always go for a nice, non-aggro hang. Intentionally don't wash your genitals. That way you know you won't have sex with whoever is coming over. It ensures you will not look thirsty **boots** by trying to get some D, P, or A the first time around. If you get a this-was-fun-we-should-do-this-again vibe, definitely wash your junk real nice the next time you kick it. My favorite spot to take people I wanna fuck but am not sure if I'm friendzoning is Jumbo's Clown Room. The girls there are technically strippers, but they really go whole hog with the gigs and sexy routines. It's always looked at as a performance because it's a novelty atmosphere. Seeing if a gay man is comfortable watching a girl drop that pussy from the ceiling to the floor on the pole in a nanosecond is really enlightening to me. If they appreciate that sensual sitches can have levity and be fun, and if they can have a good time in a hypersexualized room, they can probably have a good time in bed, too. One note: If you're a gay guy at a strip club, resist the urge to yell "Yaaaas, bitch" no matter what. Some of the foreign strippers don't get that "bitch" can be a term of endearment. The other girls may get it, but there's always that one Russian girl who don't play. (Hi, Akira! Let's do the ring toss again soon!)

If the strip club or whatever icebreaker you set up goes well, feel free to do a casual "Hey! Hands up if you like sex!" survey. There's nothing wrong with being straight up. Chances are the person you're with likes sex, 'cause who doesn't, right? So half the battle is won. Now you just have to figure out how to ask them, and if you have to keep trying to look cute when you see them, you can just be lesbefriends in sweats and a topknot.

HOW TO LOSE A TRICK

If you know you want someone gone even before they get there, turn the water off underneath the sink in the bathroom. Tell them you gotta be quick after they say they're on their way over, 'cause then they know their Cinderella is a pumpkin timer. Add that the plumber or landlord is gonna be there soon, but they were just so hot blah, blah, cock gobble, blah. Flight attendants call it a turn 'n' burn. Quick landing and then right back up into the sky. Have some Purell on standby and maybe a hand towel, two max. Don't be letting them use a big bath towel. Throw in a pair of jeans, those sheets you just fucked up, and a towel and then boom—that's a load of wash from you taking a load. No, ma'am. California has a drought and I'm doing my part.

Set a safety alarm for about five to ten minutes after they are due to arrive so you can play the fake phone call game and have an excuse to bail in case they're ugly **boots**. You can always pretend it was a voice mail from a doctor about a skin tag. Skin tag is basically an erectile-safe word.

I once accidentally made an off-color remark about color, and it made a trick leave. I had wanted him to be my fucking king. I met him on Jack'd, and he came over to explore some options. He was texting and sexting on the way over and telling me how he was gonna slam me with his BBC and telling me to get ready. So I told him he could call me Amistad 'cause I like to give rough rides to black guys. Apparently, that's racist. So now I generally try to avoid jokes like that. The only people who can acceptably say "Once you go black, you never go back" are Home Depot paint department workers who can't stress the importance of a good primer before dark colors.

Don't pry. If you see car seats, don't ask. If that dick can make a life, that dick can give you life probably. Either that or he works at a day care, which means there might be fruit snacks in the glove box. Yum. (Also… Hi, Keenan!)

The easiest way to get rid of a trick is often the one thing you forget to factor in when leaving a nightspot. Did you park in a structure? Overhead fluorescent lighting is nobody's friend, especially at 2:15 a.m. after dancing, drinking, and sweating through your shirt. Always pay first or valet, or he may decide to take a rain check.

How to **SUCK LESS** at
WHORAL SEX

25

Let's talk about how babies aren't made. If your mother woulda just been cooler about swallowing, you might not be here. Oral sex is rad. There is nothing I like more after untucking than head. My dick suffocates when it's taped to my taint, and there's no better way to revitalize it than some mouth-to-mouth resuckitation.

Sure, perfunctory childhood Popsicle training will come into play, but there's more to it than just some up-and-down **southmouthing**. It's not just about the oral. Would you go to an armless hooker? No, unless you're into that sorta thing, which is totally fine. I'd prefer a participant with hands to change a simple beej into truly whoral sex. Use your hands. A *lot*. Make it a sloppy, wet hand job with a mouth. If you wanna get fancy, g'head. Gagging on a man's penis is the most romantic thing you can do. It says "Yes, you, Mr. Man—I'm choosing your dick over oxygen right now. You're welcome." Guys love it. But not too much. If your gag reflex is too strong, just pull it out, spit back on it, get it wetter, and say something like "It's so big/hard/angry looking." If your partner still insists on skull fucking you like

This ice cream is blowjob flavored because if I eat it, that's all you're gonna get. You don't wanna fuck with this manhole after even a drop of dairy.

a watermelon, just maintain eye contact and his rapid-fire piston action will probably slow a bit. It's the same reasoning behind mobsters making someone turn away before they shoot them. It's hard to hurt someone while staring them in the eyes. Remember the end of *Sister Act*? Those mean goons just couldn't shoot Sister Mary Clarence. Deloris van Cartier *lives*!

If you're not going to take my advice about the eye contact, just shut your eyes. Balls aren't pretty. You'll find yourself drifting and thinking, "Just what the hell is that bump garden on his nuts?" Even worse, you may find your eyes drifting around the room, getting cockeyed watching that Slap Chop infomercial and wondering if those operators really are standing by, or *fuck*, did you leave clothes in the dryer? Focus. 'Cause you're gonna get back what you give out. Treat others how you want to be treated…with their mouth.

Now, I don't know much about clam digging, but I do know the couple of times I did it were fun. At first, I felt like my tongue was on a scavenger hunt, and it knew it wouldn't win but it was still going to be gung ho about it. I learned a few things down there that made me a better man, like motorboating. Motorboating is an amazing activity to do on breasts but not so much two feet south. It seems fun, but the risk of injury down there is a variable you don't want. If you give a woman really bad head, give her a gift certificate to an hour of Jet Skiing and that might make up for it. F'real. I know a bitch named Brandi who can get O-drunk on a personal watercraft and would run over a manatee if it got between her and her climax. If anyone wants to help me learn about cunnilingus more, I'll happily crowdfund an instructional video on how to be a private pussy pleaser. Donald Sutherland would be my choice to narrate it. His voice has an earnest quality but also includes the perfect amount of bass to indicate the importance of the task at hand . . . or mouth, I guess. Or wait. Do you use hands? It is like a BJ? See!? This is *exactly* why we need this. Some men, like me, are clueless.* Do you manually open a woman a little while pleasing her or dive in like a swooping seabird, mouth first? Can I really just write the alphabet with my tongue down there? First things first: We'll need to know what to call the Kickstarter. Tweet me any ideas.

Whatever gender you're servicing, try not to put your hands on the floor. That's nasty **boots**, OK? 'Cause if they're on the bed, and you're on your knees touching the floor, then touching the garden, then you're touching the garden with your mouth—not cool. I mean I'll eat a stranger's asshole, but I won't lick his floor. That's gross. Makes me wanna gag, which reminds me: Turning off your gag reflex can be done in two ways. Squeeze your left thumb. The other way is to suck that damn dick like you really wanna suck that damn dick. Get the fuck outta the damn buffet line if you're just having salad. Eat that cock and really show him how the lack of love during your childhood left a hole in your heart that only dicks and flat-screens can fill. Can't spell "happiness" without "penis," right?

GUMBALLS
(FLAVORS OF GUM THAT MIX WELL WITH BALLS)

1. Peach Trident
2. Wintergreen
3. Juicy Fruit

---

*And I've actually eaten out two different women. It's kind of a course requirement to pass health class in high school, and alcohol was involved. Tried two in one night, and the next morning I woke up and felt like someone had poured beer on my face and let it dry. One of those girls is now dead, but I'm pretty sure it had nothing to do with my performance. (Hi, Meghan, but really not 'cause you're dead.)

ORAL CARE

Now's a good time to talk about teeth, I guess. Y'know how a dumpster can be totally empty but you still wouldn't wanna go in the corners and start sniffing around? Well, your mouth operates with the same theory. Bits of old food and trash are hidden up in there, and only flossing can help. While we're at it, lemme just be blunt and say this: If you're a teenager and you're reading this, Fix your shit now! *Tell your parents you'd rather have good teeth than a car. What you drove to homecoming won't matter when you're in your twenties, but what you did with your grill will. It will make your life so much easier. No one wants to stick their genitals into that cotton-gin-lookin' jaws-of-life situation you're trying to pass off as teeth.*

I know plenty of you are reading this thinking, "Willam doesn't mean me. I just got that one snaggle. It's cool." Don't rationalize that you don't have to get it fixed 'cause it's not one of the front six or a missing molar. We all can see that black spot, and whenever I do see you, I fantasize what it would be like to put my tongue in your mouth and play with the void in your gum line, the way

you do when you lose a tooth as a kid. Then I think, "Gross. It's all rotted probably," but I still wanna do it. Maybe it's from birth, maybe it's from partying. Whatever. Some of my best friends are crackheads or have teeth like them, and that's cool. I'll still be your friend. I'll buy you a slice of pizza after the club. But if I see you buying a new car, I will ask the pertinent question, like "You didn't wanna fix that toof first, girl?" 'Cause, again, you can drive a shitty car to the club and park it blocks away so no one sees it, but you can't bring your dental danger up in there unnoticed. And if you're doing crack or meth or too many Percocets and you lose some teeth, your morals are probably questionable anyway, so why not turn a couple of tricks while you're at your rock-bottom and make the money to get your shit rigorous and right? Five hundred dollars gets that fixed. Go to a shitty neighborhood and call the dentist on the billboard by the low-income housing. You know the one. That way when we have brunch I won't think you got a raisin in your tooth when you're actually eating an omelet.

How to **SUCK LESS** at

ANAL

26

HOW TO MAKE IT A DIRTY FOUR-LETTER WORD

If you ever get to make out with me, you will immediately know exactly how I eat ass. I could get to the chicken part of a turducken with my hands tied behind my back and only using my mouth. To this day, I don't use a spoon when I eat a pudding cup. My tongue can get all the way to the bottom on its own. But before you make yourself comfortable on my face, we should make sure the patio is clean. Nothing worse that sitting on a hairy fold-up beach chair.

Don't make me eat your ass how a Gay4Pay performer eats out another guy in porn. They don't eat out. They eat around. I don't just flick a tongue to the left of the crack and hock a loogie on it, then tap it like I'm doing butthole Morse code. Douching is an essential act for going whole hog in bed. I'm talking to you, you verse tops who throw your legs up and say "OMG, I'm super wasted and think I wanna bottom"—(a) don't equate bottoming with something you have to be fucked up to do and (b) no, bitch. Get up and stumblebump your ass to the tub, sir.

James Deen gave me this shirt, and I gave him the gift of laughter. His dick and his brain are both vast.

I'm also talking to you, you vegetarians who think you don't need to clean your mudhut because you're meat-free and stay regular with leafy greens. A hole should be as pure as the snow Bambi slept on before his mom's blood fucked it all up. You too, vegans. I don't want any pole stains from your whole grains. I'm also talking to ladies and gents who took a shower in the morning and by the end of the night have their back door scents wafting up to the front door. It's nasty **boots**.

Let's start with the prep work. If you think there's a possibility of probing, eat something small beforehand. Nothing that's hard to break

The way to a man's heart is through his stomach. Since I can't cook, I usually just go in through the crawl space.

131

down, like starches or corn. Salads can be really dicey, and eggs have way too many variables. Soup is always good. No beans or dairy. The only time I've ever douched in the morning and known I'd be cool that night was when I had soup for lunch and the guy's dick was only, like, six inches.

Just for clarification, there are five levels of anal cleanliness:

1 Dugeon of Doom. Just no. It's a no. Don't go back there unless there's disaster relief on standby.

2 Stuffed Crust. The only time I say "Lemme eat your crust" is at the pizza place. So say I took a shower this morning. It's, like, eleven o'clock at night now.

3 Eat Pray Fuck. Even though you had a full meal today, you cleaned out, hope nothing gets digested, and long for a launch out the escape hatch by the time anyone wants to make that exit an entrance. Shove some soap up there in the shower and a finger or two and pray.

4 Floor Model. Good to go for fucking. You used a disposable enema, like a Fleet, or a hose a couple of times.

5 Pool Party Ass. Bitch, stick your fist in. You just had a colonic, you fasted, and you're as empty as a stepmom's promise.

Bonus **Hospitality Anus** is something that's suitable for casual—but not first—dates, bikini area grooming appointments, and especially doctor visits. Many think "Oh, lemme clean it all out for the doc," but in reality, all that water washes away the necessary bacteria to give accurate results when swabbing back there for sexually transmitted issues and potentially cancerous cells, sometimes resulting from viruses like HPV.

Now, for those about to clean your b'holes, I salute you. One would think it would be common knowledge, but more than a few ruined sheets have told tales best left in the laundry room. So y'know how you can buy those drugstore enemas prefilled? *Never* use the water in them. It has saline (salt) in it and it'll make you shit the house down. Use regular warm water, and I like to do some jumping jacks or some yoga positions and then about three to five cycles of squirt and dump. You can also get the shower attachment hose, but it can be hard to calibrate the amount of water going up there. Too much water up there and you'll breech the lower intestine, which'll make your task much harder. The goal is to clean the lower rectum. It's usually about seven to nine inches in there—cozy, but big enough for some company.

If you know you're not going to be having sex for a few hours and for sure will be eating something, take an Imodium A-D to slow down your digestive system. Live your life in the fast lane, but fuck like you're in the HOV lane.

Now, there are certain times when you don't want to even try with an ass. If the hookup is especially hot or a straight guy wants to try getting dicked for a minute, give it a go. But the minute you get even a snifference the room's stinking, you pull out and get out. I've been in cuddle puddles that got muddy, and there's no denying or hoping that that particular shit whiff will go away.

I've been out when I'm 95 percent sure I wouldn't be getting any but still kept that 5 percent chance alive with smart after-hour food choices. Instate the just-the-tip rule. Order some fries and eat just the tips. It's weird enough that he can ask what you're doing and you're probably shameless enough to reply with a wink that you only like the tip. It's actually really helpful, because the best parts of the fries are the crunchy tips and the middles usually are soft. If he finds your flirty fry answer charming enough to advance to the bonus just-the-tip round, your ass should still be good to go.

If the ass play isn't in the cards not because of some fault of your own, there's not much I can tell you. I once fucked around with a guy who was six feet eight, and the second he pulled his pants down, I knew I wasn't gonna shit right for a week. You'd think I'd love elephantitis of the cock, but sometimes it's just too much. You want a sensible portion of dick, not the size that requires

you to get a full-on colonic and fast for a week prior. Other times, I've literally said to guys "I'm on PrEP but I'm not prepped if you know what I mean." They knew it was gonna be very proceed at your own risk, and I knew to get off as soon as they got it in because I knew the booty bombs could start in T-minus six inches.

Tops don't think about this kinda stuff, and it sucks when someone asks you to hang out and you think it might be for sex and then they're like "Let's go eat," but you know if you do, you won't be able to get fucked good later. So you order some food and play with it. Maybe you eat a couple of bites and you know your douche is dunzo. Then when Mr. Man later wants to hit it, just give him the look like he's a coach passenger waiting for the first-class toilet. Like he saw what was going into your mouth and he knows where it's gonna end up. Insensitive tops will never learn. Have sex, then get a goddamned snack. It makes much more sense for a date. I can get behind that. And by that I mean I can really just get in front of that with my leg on your coffee table.

Getting a leg up while cleaning out can also be useful. Commode positioning seems weird to talk about, but it's often left out of the equation. Squatting on the toilet allows muscles to relax in a way that sitting on it and trying to expel the water can't allow. The Squatty Potty is a great tool for that, but so is just standing on the rim of the bowl like a toilet gargoyle.

In other instances, your hole might need a holiday. Sometimes the day after I've been fucked, it feels to me like I'm about to give birth to a butt baby made of thumbtacks each time I try to poop. Add some mild razor burn to that sometimes and it's not a party anyone in their right mind would want to crash. Closures due to pipe damage are a fact of life.

Lack of lube can sometimes inflict damage. It is as important to sex as fire is to cooking. If you don't have lube and you still want to fuck, spit works well but keep reapplying. I fucked my way through most of Europe and ran out of lube somewhere around Belgium, and spit was my savior. I wasn't happy just backpacking through the old country. I went buttpacking. (I also stole that joke from a nice lady named Producer Coinslot.)

Please don't try to fuck me with a packet of lube. That's like having McDonald's condiments at a White House dinner. My ass should be treated like a municipal holiday. Don't disrespect my picnic area. That includes the swimming hole, too. The iconic pool sex scene in *Showgirls* lasts less than thirty seconds, and that's probably a good thing because fucking in water is a bad idea for women. It strips the natural lubricant their vaginas are nice enough to create for them. Men aren't lucky enough to have any glands back there to secrete fuck juice, so it's an even worse idea for them. Plus, it's super disrespectful to future swimmers. Like sticking your whole fist into a bowl of communal salsa. Party foul.

This isn't salsa, but you get the idea.

As a stand-up type of citizen who likes to sit down on lotsa things, I'd like to stress that love is not a prophylactic. I don't care if he loves you. Make him wear a rubber. If he buys you stuff, then maybe he can hit it raw. Just make sure one of the things he pays for is a prescription for PrEP. I mean you can top all you want without getting HIV like 99-ish percent, but bottoming is still risky biz if you're rawdogging. PrEP lets you live out your fantasy life with little or no penance after. It makes it almost OK to get pulled into a bathroom stall and have your foot slip into the toilet, soaking your shoe, while being pinned up against a wall that's never been washed. I'm not saying don't use condoms at all, but now when a condom breaks, I don't worry that every time I sneeze for the month following that I'm seroconverting. I mean I wouldn't go whole hog and start treating my body like an unlicensed sperm bank, but I definitely feel a little freer to do my thing.

There's the school of thought that if the condom doesn't break, you ain't fucking hard enough. I can sometimes get down with some rough stuff, but I think the term "struggle snuggle" is a way nicer way of saying "Fuck me like an *SVU* episode." To me, it's way safer to do that kinda stuff with safe words and in well-lit rooms, because if you're tied up, lotsa weird shit can go down. I was bound and gagged once for a B&D sesh and thought a guy was penetrating me, so I started rolling around like Sonic the Hedgehog.

He undid the restraints and I told him how uncool it was that he was trying to stick it in raw, but he countered with holding his foot up and telling me it was his big toe. I was toe raped, you guys. In retrospect, I would've felt his Prince Albert piercing, so I know he wasn't lying. (Hi, Damien!)

Next time I saw that guy was at a bathhouse, and that was even crazier. Those places are like Space Mountain: dark with many dangerous choices. I mostly mean the porno mazes where you can walk right into a wall and stub your toe or cut your foot. Blood sometimes happens during sex if you're a gay man. If you bleed after sex, it's not always something to worry about. It's fuckin' gross, but not enough to make you call 911. It's either a tear from rough intercourse or the baby Jesus weeping tears of blood through your asshole. He's like "I told you. Water into wine, fags."

This one particularly bountiful day in NYC, I fucked a guy in the gym for breakfast, got splashed with a protein shake after a day about town, and then had a sensible fuck for dinner.

TOP TALK

Bottom to top, me to you. Here are some things I should mount above a headboard:

▉ *Every thrust's endgame should not be to herniate a disc. You can get all jackhammer with it eventually, but breaking and entering shouldn't be your MO. Put your dick on the porch of the house and say hi. Then go in the back door. Let that ass know there's a visitor by throbbing or flexing your dick a few times. Consider this a foyer minute. After you see the bottom is cool, g'head and head to pound town.*

▉ *If you see your bottom is taking a hit of poppers/amyl, please allow him the moment of resealing it before you go apeshit on his hole. Then fuck him good enough that if he sneezes the next day, it'll make his butthole hurt.*

▉ *Approved objects only. There is no need to put your fingers in while your dick is, or worse so, your toe. This little piggy stayed the fuck home.*

▉ *I am not just a hole. I have front parts, too. Chances are I may also want to get off.*

▉ *I know. You hate condoms. But wearing one is easier than convincing me you love me in hopes that I'll let you skip that step.*

Afterward, I was in the shower and I was like "Fuck. This is the third time today you washed your ass, Willam." And then I was like "Damn. You fucked three different guys. You shoulda had the forethought to call down to reception to get more towels." But also #whore. And then I told myself back, "No, girl. Whores get paid. You're a slut." Then, as I dried myself with the corner of the bathmat, I reminded myself, "Don't be so hard on yourself, myself." It coulda been four guys in actuality, but I had sent one home who did *not* look like his pic. I'm not trying to say everyone needs to be the little engine that could and pull a train, but if you do, I'm here to advise you to always allow a fifteen-minute gap. Don't be ashamed to admit that it's been an active night either. Sure, it's a double-down risk. When it's getting real hot and heavy with that third or fourth guy, you may wanna try to test the waters, telling them that they're the hottest you've had all day. If they ask, say you've tried it with a few others today and just was feeling some kinda way.

Now, it can go one of two ways: He can say "Oooh, hot. You're fuckin' nasty. Lemme get you pregnant." Or he can say "Excuse me while I remove my penis because you are an actual waste can." Either is fine. The judgment is not. Don't feel bad. No one can make you feel any way that you don't want to about yourself. One guy, who wasn't my first partner of the day, told me I shoulda told him before he came over, and he started asking if I had been tested recently. I should just get a ticker tape for my headboard. BREAKING NEWS: NO ONE CARES. I was safe and I knew what I was doing with my body, so I was cool about it. "Did he give me something?" should never pop into your head, because you should be asking yourself, "Did I allow myself to get exposed to something?" It takes two. Nobody *gives* you anything. You get it on your own. I like to hammer this point home with everyone, because it's about being in total control of yourself. That's why at each show I give out condoms (with my picture on them) as a preventive measure. Not only does the lucky individual think "What would Willam do?" before using it, or not (FYI, I'd fuckin' suck it), but they also know I practice what I preach. You

SEXTING

Sexting the wrong person can be a bitch. Work quickly to resolve it. Google spam and start posting some random weird shit combined with porn so people won't know what's up with your account. Write up something about wiring money to Angola for an ambassador or some shit. Say your phone was stolen or your nephew got it. Everybody's got that one bastard kid in their family whose mother gave him too many sweets instead of side eyes and slaps.

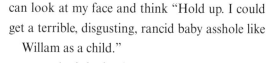

can look at my face and think "Hold up. I could get a terrible, disgusting, rancid baby asshole like Willam as a child."

And that's why I say to most girls in the audience "There's a six-pack available in the lobby for ten dollars." I especially say it to you, dear reader. You should get the family pack. I mean I was an unplanned baby. My parents had sex after installing a linoleum floor. I think that's why I'm so down-to-earth. See what I did there?

Can you imagine raising someone who thinks that this is OK? That's the risk you take each time you have unprotected sex, ladies.

Available now at WillamBelli.com.org.gov.

HOW TO REMOVE LUBE FROM ANYTHING

I learned about this because I fucked some dude at a hospice when I was nineteen. (I wasn't Tranna-Nicole-Smithing. He worked there as a janitor.) He could get anything offa anything, including me. To get lube off your body is a three-step process that I have to be super fastidious about because my tucking tape won't stick if there's any lubricant left. First, wipe away any excess **mudhoney**. Next step is a good cleansing (I like Dove soap). Rinse and then rub dry with a paper towel or rag. Then repeat the wash and rinse, and you should be good to go.

The most effective way to remove silicone lube not on your skin is with regular liquid dish soap applied, then rinsed. For machine-washable sheets and fabrics, spot-clean first with soap, then rinse thoroughly. Once you have spot-treated the item, get your maid to wash normally. Don't dry in a machine. Allow the item to air dry like that scene in The Color Purple where Whoopi and her sister fuck up all the nice hanging laundry. Verify that the silicone spot is gone; if not, repeat. Once the spot has been removed, you may use the dryer as appropriate.

For flooring or surfaces, be extremely careful, because silicone is slippery and spreads easily. Use the same process as with fabrics. If it's a laptop, find a fat guy or a fag at the Apple Store. They'll definitely help you outta solidarity because they probably jerk off the most and know all about being a crumbdump and/or cumdumpster.

How to **SUCK LESS** at
COMING OUT

Teenagers hit me up online at least once a day, seeking assistance with coming out. Usually, I know they're gay just by their thumbnail pics, and chances are the people they're about to tell do, too. BTW: If your closet door has bead curtains, you can probably skip disclosing you're a homosexual to your parents. You're so gay you fart with a lisp.

So there's no need to be nervous. Nerves are wasted energy. It's borrowing trouble before it's there. Get excited about the future instead of worrying. Plan a beautiful little day when you know who's ever important in your life will be present for 10 min. Keep it quick. Your Dad really doesn't wanna miss the game because he thinks he needs to play Father of the Year and let his son who he probably had an idea was gay years ago properly do it and get it out.

My parents told me on a Friday night about my two aunts and uncles being LGBT, and all I remember is trying to continually grab the remote. I wanted to watch *Family Matters*, not listen to family matters.

Coming out is a piece of cake. Literally. Bake a fuckin' cake. Don't go to a superstore bakery. Sheet cakes are shit cakes.

But, yeah. Back to you being a fag/dyke/trans. Get a cake. My parents, despite being television Nazis, were the best ever to deal with because their family tree already had so many LGBT entries on it. They probably had an idea I wasn't straight because I'd made it clear I was going to marry at least one member of either Judas Priest or NKOTB (Funny that Rob Halford and Jon Knight ended up coming out too). My mom says she knew when I was three because I used child safety scissors to cut some suspenders I didn't like off my pants. She told my father I was gay and he just laughed. Cut to him taking me to *Rocky Horror Picture Show* and sleeping in the car to take me home at three a.m.

By seventh grade, I wore a gay pride necklace in my school photo and was the only out kid all through high school. I also had a family member walk in on me sucking dick, and that was an easy way to come out to the other half of my family. That's what cousins are for, right? Boy cousins do that kinda thing, weird as it sounds. I had one who "made" me blow him, and it's not as weird as one would think now that I'm an adult. Granted, he's dead now, so I don't have to deal with any tense looks while I have a hot dog at family functions, but generally, incest is fine as long as babies can't be made and it's consensual.

Telling your parents you're bisexual or gender fluid is very in right now and keeps the options open if you change your mind or science comes up with something fun. I did the bi thing, but only in AOL chat rooms when they allowed thirty-one people in them at a time. I was always jealous of people who could "pass" as straight until I realized I had nothing to be ashamed about. It's like what Magneto says to Mystique in *X-Men*. Should a tiger hide its stripes? No.

That's why it infuriates me when people wait to come out and then get celebrated. There's a kid from *Glee* who could've easily come out at the height of his show's success, but he chose to stay in his plush closet and presumably whisper his secrets into a hot Brazilian's asshole. It's people like this who make me worry for kids, because if there's nothing wrong with being gay, why aren't they open? Then when they come out, we give them magazine covers. I think famous people who are enjoying gay sex while excluding the parts of their lives that may indicate their sexual preference should have to pick up trash at the end of the Pride parade. Caitlyn can drive the trash truck provided she's learned to drive in heels, and Shane, Joey, and the fags from *Teen Wolf* can all deal with the bins.

Remember Wentworth Miller? Imagine if he came out while he was on a Fox show and how that coulda changed the landscape years earlier. Sure, he was worried about never working again, but I think his acting pretty much sealed that fate. I understand needing to be able to disappear into a role as an actor, but denying something that's not bad only furthers the assumption that it's worthy of shame. Staying in the closet makes it seem like there's something wrong with being you, and there's nothing wrong with you except maybe that one toe you have that looks funny in sandals.

The weird toe is probably a genetic thing, much like any deviations from a heteronormative predisposition. If someone in your family doesn't like how you're shaping up, let them know their options. They can evolve or they can be cut from your life. You cannot allow yourself to be treated poorly by others just because you're related and they're "family." Surround yourself with people who treat you how you want to be treated. If you can't live your life a certain way because you won't get the support you need financially or something, you have to make the tough decision of how important being you is to you. My parents were scared as fuck about me going out on my own, but they didn't have much choice because they weren't financing me at that point. I knew I wanted outta my small hometown

This is my best friend DJ Pasta Body and my other best friend Courtney's freakshow foot.

at twelve, and I had my first job bussing tables at a lesbian-owned bakery brunch spot and saved every penny. If you can look in the mirror at night and lay your head down knowing that you were true to you, then you did good—and if you can lie down in bed and look in the mirror at the same time, congrats. You're probably in my room.

If you're a budding homosexual *and don't want to come out, at least align yourself with the popular, pretty girls, because they will most likely date the boys who are most likely to torment you and they won't tolerate their mates bullying their fruity friend.*

How to **SUCK LESS** at
HAVING A NICE HOME

28

My husband once told me all he really needed was a hot plate and a shitter. I tend to think the same but with, like, maybe a dartboard and a mirror, too. The one thing that most everyone can agree on is that cleaning sucks. So keeping it simple will help it suck less, which may lead to getting sucked more, because nobody wants to have sex in a pigpen. I mean I will, but I'd rather not, y'know?

Here's a quick list to make your home clean-ish when you're about to have company. I call it Operation Transvestite Storm.

1 Hit the head and squirt that blue toilet cleaner shit under around the rim. TBC…

2 Kitchen: Hide/do/throw out the dishes. Grab the toaster, which you turned on its side to make grilled cheese, and tip it back upright (toldya it was a great tip).

Pillow choices say a lot about a person. A poor choice would be moving my pillows or furniture in my house. The stains live there and like to be left alone.

3 Get rid of any pet hair. No one wants to sit on your couch covered in hair. Either throw a blanket over it (not a sheet, 'cause *ewwww*) or use painters' tape to lift it off. If you have wood floors, I've totally just blow-dried my floors with a hair dryer, 'cause it basically acts like a leaf blower and gets the hair into a more general pile faster than sweeping.

4 Go back to the toilet. Now try to power-wash that *kersplat* of crap off the side that looks like a Rorschach test made of poop. Pee real hard on it. If that doesn't work or you can't pee standing up, a traditional toilet brush will do the job. I usually just use my sock to wipe up any splashage or piss on the rim, 'cause I'm kinda a pig. Oh. Clean the mirror while you're there, too. The water drip marks and **residont** from popped pimples on a medicine cabinet mirror are even grosser when they're not your own.

5 Light a candle in the bathroom. I know I'd rather shit in a yard than have anyone smell my booty bounty, and the sulfur

145

from a lit match is the best way to cover it. "Did someone smoke in here?" is always a better question than "Did someone have turkey chili?"

6 **Fluff the pillows** and make sure some surface area is visible on whatever kinda table you have. Even if it's some milk crates and an old door. Think HGTV, not *Hoarders*.

7 **Pick cigarette butts** out of any plants.

In a bathroom, anything guests may need should be out: extra toilet paper, a towel, or maybe a Dyson Airblade if you're bougie. Don't be going into my restroom and coming out with a new hair tie and a different colored eye shadow on. Dipping up into my makeup is *no*. Maybe a squirt of lotion, but don't even look at the La Mer. That's not for you. If my stuff is out, try to avoid it, and just shit and run. Bathrooms should be streamlined and German in disposition. Bathrooms should not fuck around in the least.

Making a large wall into a focal point doesn't necessarily mean you have to fill it up with a buncha shit. I regularly print and cut out video game graphic icons and throw them up on a blank wall to change up the look. There is power in negative space.

No one I know really has time to decorate. It just sorta happens as you live in a space. I had an interior designer once when I bought my first house, and I ended up hating him and all his ideas except for an awesome couch. I'm a Cancer, so that means my home is very important to me, which explains why I may have also gotten into a fistfight with the designer for trying to make my dining room look like the Wynn. Keep it simple and ease up on the tchotchkes, 'cause you'll just have to move them all and dust and then move them back. I have an aversion to a buncha crap because my parents saved everything. Like, why does anyone need my old report cards? So I bit a kid and have a problem with authority. Nothing new there.

Think of the wear and tear that goes on versus how much effort you want to spend cleaning. My white walls in my living room were no match for the giant beast that liked to sleep against them in the same spot by the air vent in the floor so I had to paint them all gray. My husband suggested we just

do the one wall but I told him accent walls are for lazy faggots. The dog's fatness even corroded the copper on the pennies that I put on the wall at my house. At a certain point you just say "fuck it" though, right?

These are above my friend Leo's bed. The Lady Bunny one is useful for whenever he wants to hold off from cumming too quickly. I usually think of my grandma and mayonnaise when I need to hold off so Bun Bun is a fair equivalent I guess.

Flick her vagina and speak to her in whale.

As a big fan of a little choking action, I'm used to rough **trade** *putting me in a half-nelson, but being on this Paris wall next to half a Nelson is just as good. @Surianiart can whip up any kinda art for your wall to funk up your home a bit.*

Pictures should be on the walls, because you want to keep surfaces open for your guests to not use a coaster or engage in spontaneous coffee table sex. No one ever said "I can't wait to invite people over and show off the magnificent grain of this wood furniture." Being precious with your things makes having fun super hard. The most common example of this is having a buncha clutter in your bedroom. No family photos. It should be a lewdness sanctuary with more lube than a Pep Boys. Maybe a dresser. No chairs, though. Take it from me, the only place to sit down in my bedroom is my face. If you're confused as to what should go into your home, get real fucked up and visit an IKEA. See which mock living space you gravitate toward and take notes before security asks you to leave. Then just go get Swedish meatballs and eat, like, two before you figure out they're from Costco. I like customizing light switches and outlet covers too, because it's an easy change back should you move or change your mind.

The easiest way to make any space more welcoming is by getting a plant. They naturally deodorize that staleness of the beer you spilled on the rug that you then just flipped over. Plus, they're green. Green is good. It inspires money, brings calm (hence greenrooms backstage), and will make you look like a responsible adult if you don't kill it. An easy way to add levels to your rooms is by hanging a plant from the ceiling near a corner. I've had this one unkillable plant called a philodendron for over three years. They're usually sold in pots with wires twisted into a hook at the top so you can just hang it and go. I have cactuses because they're the only thing my dog Warner won't eat.

My mom always told me to keep an aloe plant by the door in case I ever got burned in the kitchen, but I mainly use the pointy stalks to clean out my pipes and one-hitters. It's a great porch plant.

I'm obsessed with AHS *(American Horror Story). Bestiality on primetime. God Bless Ryan Murphy.*

How to **SUCK LESS** at

ROOMMATES

29

Plants are the easy thing. They don't talk back. People do. One of my housemates inspired me to name my Internet connection Error Connect 'cause they were always downloading shit that made my browsing slower than his share of the rent. These cohabitational issues can be tricky, but so can the people your housemates bring home to fuck. *Never* leave valuables out. I had a March of Dimes bottle stolen from my kitchen by a one-night stand and was really saddened by it because I also had some quarters in there. I walked in on my first roommate naked on a futon in the living room with some hot dude eating a cup of noodles and didn't know what to be more upset about: that the hot guy was eating my fucking soup or that their buttholes were all over the communal seating area after they'd fucked. I used to use his electric beard trimmer to shave my balls, though, so everything evened out in the end.

If you're particular about where anuses should and shouldn't go, maybe fly solo. Especially don't live with someone if you're not OK with the bathroom not being exactly like how you left it. My bathroom ranges in cleanliness from spotless on Fridays when Blanca comes to somewhere around a nice Citgo or Kmart restroom. Seeing the evidence all over the bowl that the struggle was real damn real for someone else is kinda nasty, but whatcha gonna do about it? You can either talk to them about it or use one of their towels to clean it up, depending on how over it you are. I'm a terrible roommate. I'm the kinda bitch who will wake someone up with an empty ice cream carton I pulled from the trash can, yelling *"Did you eat my ice cream?"* even though I know the answer is yes. Tables being turned, I'm sure I would stand right up for my actions and claim your fat ass didn't need it. Either way, I will wear a red dress to my roommate's funeral and throw the empty Ben & Jerry's tub onto the coffin as it lowers into the grave.

I tend to think the best roommates are platonic boys and girls. There's always some sorta

Does anyone wanna come home to this?

underlying competition with two gay guys or two girls or two straight boys. Like, even with me and mine, who have nothing to compete over because we're different body types who like different types of men, we still find stuff to top each other on. The other day he farted with his door open and the following ensued:

WILLAM: I dunno if you're trying to compete with me or what, but my morning bed farts were iconic compared to your squeakers.

PASTABODY: Well, that's funny, 'cause you heard mine but I didn't hear yours.

WILLAM: No, that's just acoustics 'cause my room is bigger. One thing is for sure. You def smelt mine. My fragrance is legendary.

PASTABODY: Gross. No.

WILLAM: Well, we'll just have to see what the judges say.

Then I farted so hard I had to throw out a pair of sweats. Communication is key, right after not soiling yourself. Those kinda morning conversations are sometimes all that's tolerable. Like, if someone says "G'morning" and I don't say anything back, that's a good indication to move on, right? But some persist with chirping akin to the faggotty Snow White birds. "How'd you sleep?" "What's wrong?" "Are you in a bad mood?" Here's the deal: If you have to ask if I'm in bad mood, the answer is always either "Yes," "No comment," or "Bitch, I might be." Again: communication. If you can't do it, do yourself a favor and be more successful by allowing yourself to live on your own. Even a passive-aggressive fridge Post-it note with "Mine" written on it counts as an attempt to communicate, so baby steps, I guess. Here are some things that it might help to know about each other:

Living with someone is *waaaaay* easier when there are two bathrooms. Otherwise, I find myself mad at stupid stuff, like why is my soap wet? I don't want my soap wet until I want to take a shower. So if you like someone 90 percent and 10 percent of the things they do annoy you, remember it decreases by 10 percent incrementally, with a shared shitter making the approval rating 80 percent. That's a C. That means 20 percent or one-fifth of the time you're home you run the risk of wanting to sit in your room with your door shut, which will only lead other occupants to believe you're either a manic depressive, an ISIS member, or just a chronic masturbator.

YOUR SHIT SHACK AIN'T A LIBRARY LIST (MAGAZINES TO SHIT TO)

- **Highlights**
- **AAA's *Via* magazine.** *It's the auto club travel mag. Great for if your dad comes over to poop.*
- **Playboy.** *It'll make people go "Playboy? Why he got* Playboy? *Maybe he's bi. Oooh, I wonder if he tops."*

- *Lastly, I implore you not to put* **Vanity Fair** *in your bathroom. Everything is too long and you'll have hemorrhoids by the time you hafta flip to page 216 to continue the article. Instead, use the equally gender-neutral* **Entertainment Weekly** *and stay up to date on what's ~~pooping~~ popping in culture.*

PUT YOUR TRASH CAN in a corner so you can use the wall as a lazy way to pile an extra day or so worth of shit in there because you're a fuckin' pig.

Don't be one of those people who poops with the window shut. If you want to mask the sound of your booty bounty bursting forth, run the cold water, 'cause landlords usually pay for that. I've heard some people turn a blow-dryer on, but that's an electrical drain and greenhouse-effects your bathroom into a hot chamber of ass. If the ass won't evaporate from the air upon flushing, you can always pull out the window screen and use it as a fan to waft that scent. I've been in shit-uations where I even tried opening up the cabi-nets to trap some of the stank air in there. I keep matches in there to eliminate that issue.

I don't recommend bringing electronics into the bathroom. Otherwise your MacBook Air runs the risk of turning into a craptop. Water, poop, fluids, and aerosols are really not awesome for your devices. I've dropped my phone in the toilet. It's not something you ever wanna hafta fish out. Slippery little sucker.

MOVING TIP

The smartest thing you can do when relocating to a new city is to get a grasp on your surroundings ASAP. Like, doing a lap at a party as soon as you get there so you can scope everything out. My advice is, if you're hot, get a rich guy to take you out on a date and ask him for a helicopter tour of the city. Let him suck you off while you watch porn too, 'cause that's the right thing to do. Just saying.

If you're ugly, just get a shower curtain with a map of your new town on it so you can look at it while you poop. You probably spend a lot of time in the bathroom anyway, what with the crying in the bathtub and/or jerking off over the sink.

REASONS YOU MIGHT THINK ARE OK TO HAVE SEX IN YOUR ROOMMATE'S ROOM BUT ACTUALLY AREN'T

■ *'Cause you ain't done sheets in a minute and you don't want the hookup to find pieces of Teddy Grahams cookies.*

■ *'Cause your comforter smells like a comfarter.*

■ *'Cause your roomie has Apple TV and you can play the good porn on his flat-screen.*

■ *'Cause they have that one big mirror that makes everything look like life-size porn.*

■ *'Cause you let your dog sleep in your bed with you.*

PISS BETTER

AT LEAST WIPE

ASSHOLE

Fold on dotted lines, put some chewed-up gum GUM ← *there so it sticks*

Rip this page out!

How to **SUCK LESS** at
THROWING PARTIES

To determine your guest list, just divide the square footage of your party space by the number of people you could end up in bed with, and that's how many people you invite. Bartenders are great options, too. Hire your fave from the local bar for a hundred dollars or so and it's a good solid, I'd say, 65 to 80 percent chance he will fuck you or one of your guests. Bartenders are town bicycles, and just like bikes, they have ten speeds: slut, whore, player, hooker, skank, nympho, floozy, hussy, humpdog, and flirt.

You don't want people in and out of your fridge and freezer all night. If you invite more than thirty people, really think about hiring some help. If I do more than fifty people, I usually hire two bartenders. Drunk people seem to forget that even toilets can only serve one asshole at a time. This one dude I try to fuck every time I'm in Chicago, named Art, said, "A thirsty friend is more dangerous than a vengeful friend." I don't understand that, but I do know if it's ever his birthday, I'm gonna just shove a Pop-Tart on a stripper's dick and tell him to blow that. No one actually ever eats the cake because carbs are the enemy of getting drunk.

If hiring professionals isn't in the budge, you need to round up your two besties and institute a four-drink maximum until at least two hours of the party have elapsed. Assign each a role. One person on analysis (playlists, parking, running interference on neighbors/cops/pets) and the other on paralysis (booze, drugs, maybe a snack or two). If they don't wanna help, they're dicks. Try asking people you've known for seven years, because if a friendship lasts seven years, studies show it's probably for the long run (I forget what studies, but I know for sure I read it in something). If you haven't known anyone in your town for seven years, ask people you've seen naked. If you don't have anyone at your party you've seen naked, kill yourself (or just turn up the heat; it'll make people disrobe faster). Put extra bags of ice in the bathroom, hidden behind the shower curtain because it's always the first thing to run out, too. Having the tub filled will also keep people from fucking in the tub or pissing in it when the toilet backs up from too many flushes.

BGB: BYE GIRL BYE

▦ *When you're the smartest person in the room, it's time to leave the room (another lesson I learned from a girl group).*

▦ *Call the cops on your own party. Great way to clear out assholes and stragglers.*

▦ *If "No Scrubs" comes on, leave immediately after. It's not gonna get better than that.*

▦ *Put out some hummus and ten minutes later say the toilet just broke. Everyone will be like "Bye!"*

SUCKLESS AT SOUNDS

SOIREE EDITION

Think of a movie without music. It would be real damn boring. Music is an important way to set the tone, underscoring and advancing your party along. Shutting it down is also the best way to indicate to guests that it's time to GTF out. You want the kinda songs people know the lyrics to but they actually butcher them. The kinda songs you can't help but nod your head to.

"Candy Shop" *50 Cent*

"Lemme Freak" *Lil Dicky*

"Ladies' Night" *Missy Elliott*

"Holiday" and/or "Beautiful Stranger" *Madonna*

"Oops!...I Did It Again" *Britney*

"Bend Ova" *Lil Jon featuring Tyga*

"All About That Bass" *Meghan Trainor*

"Doo-Wop (That Thing)" *Lauryn Hill*

"Thrift Shop" *Macklemore featuring Ryan Lewis*

"Super Freak" *Rick James*

"Black Magic" *Little Mix*

"It's Gonna Be a Lovely Day" *S.O.U.L. S.Y.S.T.E.M. featuring Michelle Visage*

"Don't (Rick Ross Remix)" *Ed Sheeran*

"Any Way You Want It" *Journey*

"All Cried Out" *Blonde featuring Alex Newell*

"Legendary" *Alaska Thunderfuck*

"Start Me Up" *Rolling Stones*

"I Am the Body Beautiful" *Salt-N-Pepa*

"You Make Me Feel (Mighty Real)" *Sylvester*

"Brenda Had a Baby" *Tupac*

"Sweet Thing" *Rufus featuring Chaka Khan*

"Primadonna Girl" *Marina and the Diamonds*

"Thank You" *Busta Rhymes*

"What's New Pussycat?" *Tom Jones*

"I Want It That Way" *Backstreet Boys*

"Headband" *B.o.B featuring 2 Chainz*

"Coin on the Dresser" *Willam*

2.

PARTY GAMES

1 Battleshots. *Pizza box, shot glasses, Sharpie. Get the good marker you can huff, too.*

2 Dirty Jenga. *Spin the Bottle crossed with Truth or Dare.*

3 Scattergories. *Shit on a twister mat and spin around in it. Great for Scat Parties or Earth Day.*

4 A good ol' ho stroll. *No pads. Day face. Faux hooking. See what you and your sister can do on that one strip of the street where the cars slow down. Winner wins bragging rights and possibly a ride.*

3.

WILLAM

SUCKING LESS AT HALLOWEEN

Halloween is make-or-break time. The right getup can showcase that you're clever and creative, and it will get you laid in one fell swoop. Just putting on red underwear and saying you're the devil is lame. You're not. You're the devil because you "forget" to mention your genital herpes to hookups. Think of something topical that also won't make you the douche in the club who keeps smacking people at every move with your stupid angel wings or giant cardboard box. It's also not the time to attempt something that will eat up time when you could be having fun. I saw too many attempts at Lady Gaga cheek prosthetics in 2011 and most ended up looking like they had pot stickers glued to their faces.

A lot of folks tell me "I wanna be you for Halloween, but I can't fit seven dicks in my mouth. What should I do?" Well, here are some quickie looks for people who know that calling their drag queen friend to help them on the 30th is like calling Jesus to help dye Easter eggs. I'm fuckin' busy. Don't try it, Mary. Halloween is a drag queen high holiday. Girls aren't the only ones who can ditch their dignity on October 31. I got you, guys. Turn the page.

If anyone asks if you're the Tin Man, tell them you're dressed as Slutty Mercury Poisoning.

This is the IDGAF skeleton. Get a friend to draw it out. This one took Raja all of five minutes.

A tater thot jock is a great way to let people know that they could potentially be your Mr. or Mrs. Potato Head. Overcook them in the oven so they dry out on low heat. You want them as thirsty as you.

Continuing with the guys-can-be-whores-too theme, I present a hipster vampire. Just throw a blood collection vial on a chain with a bloody tampon to suck for the pictures.

This is inspired by my manager, David, who looks like a sweet little bear but in actuality is a pimp who provides pussy across the land. Teddy Ruxpimp is a classic. All you need is bear-related paraphernalia, a name tag, and a cassette tape affixed to your chest.

Halloween is the most common day when heteros wade into LGBT waters. We have better parties. Point-blank. Ergo, this is prime time to bag a straight guy. It won't be reciprocal, or even sanitary in most cases, but it will be enjoyable.

If you're a gay boy, pick a country (Hi, UKers!) and paint your face like their flag. It's a good convo starter, so when the guy in the bathroom line asks, "What are you?" you can reply, "I'm the fag of England." Nine times outta ten, he'll probably say, "Flag or fag?" and you can reply with "Either-or" and a wink. The wink will relay that you're open for biz should he wanna test the waters. He also may want to punch you, and that means he's not into it...yet. Use lots of liquor to wash away that thin line between gay bashing and hate fucking. If he's with his girl, it's always easy to make her the target and then bait and switch. Girls like to make out with anyone when they're drunk, especially drag queens, so take advantage of that. If he keeps saying that he's with his woman, go with the subtle "That's cool. Somebody hasta hold the camera."

PS: Dumpsters always smell like piss. Don't blow people near them even if it's garbage for a nice store like Burdines or Radio Shack.

I had a Zombie Princess Di look planned for the first episode of **Drag Race** *with the Apocalypse challenge but was told not to do it, so I saved it for this. Poor judgment really can stand the test of time.*

How to **SUCK LESS** at

CONTROLLED SUBSTANCES

Now, I'm not saying you should sneak drugs into any situation where they're not allowed. Remember, inner beauty doesn't get drink tickets, so BYOB, bitch.

HAIR BOTTLE

*W*hat you'll need. If you're trying to sneak a bottle in because you're poor, this is an awesome option. If this isn't possible due to no one on your crew having long hair, you may just have to buttchug before you get inside and rely on your buzz staying strong enough to avoid going to the bar for three hours or so. I know I previously mentioned buttchugging, but disposable enemas also work great as contraband-smuggling receptacles and a way to sneak G or any other liquid onto a cruise. Y'know how anyone with drugs can upsell their product by, like, 200 percent because of the limited supply and high demand? Nix that. Forget about the high bar costs, too.

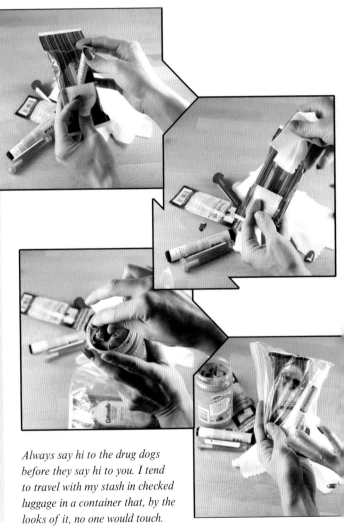

Always say hi to the drug dogs before they say hi to you. I tend to travel with my stash in checked luggage in a container that, by the looks of it, no one would touch.

SKIP THIS PART, MOM

I'm just putting this here because no one has ever started a story with "Oh my god, this one time I was having the funnest salad." No, bitch. Get high. At least once in your life.

If you don't have rolling papers or want to risk catching Alzheimer's by puff-puff passing outta a tin can, try ripping out a page in the Bible. Consider it like a holy ghost kinda smoke.

Like a baby Tostito Scoop, but for drugs.

I like to use blunt papers or cut up a Swisher Sweet or Philly. You can lightly moisten it with a spray bottle if it's too brittle.

This is why I could never transition, 'cause I know if I did, I'd definitely have some ho-length acrylics on 24/7 and couldn't roll blunts as tight as I do. I dunno how Latrice does it. (Hi, Latrice!)

This is also a great reason to keep a fireplace lighter on hand because nothing says crackhead like burned thumbnails. Fuck flying. If I could chose a superpower it would be a Bic finger. Imagine being able to light your bong just by pointing at it. Nothing says I don't have custody of my kids more so than a yellowy singed acrylic thumbnail corner. Also, don't leave a pinky nail long for your bumps. Just use a key, Einstein. Drug habits should never dictate grooming.

Sativa

Indica

If it's 4:20am, don't smoke a sativa. Sativas are head highs that give you euphoric pep and creativity along with an uptick in alertness. The indica strain is helpful with relaxation/sleep & pain relief and will make you into a hamburglar, appetite-wise.

Stoner Boners

*Female drug dealers are always more reliable. They also have more places to hide the product.

Indica = In da Couch

* Most edibles are Indicas, which is why they can knock you the fuck out.

Creative Energy

Pain/Appetite

BONUS DRUGS

UPPERS

Cocaine, Crack, Ecstasy, Meth, Adderall.

iTunes: Avicii, Calvin Harris, Diplo

Next step: 5-HTP to make the come-down easier.

DOWNERS

Xanax, Valium, Alcohol, Vicodin, Oxy, Heroin.

iTunes: anything 90's

Next step: Netflix & chill pills.

I try to vape mostly but will treat myself to a blunt when necessary. I swore off smoking as a habit when my Baltimore PD uncle was diagnosed with throat cancer. He survived and now uses a machine to assist with speaking. And he's still a policeman. They call him Robocop. (Hi, Uncle Scott!)

I'm lucky to live in LA, but most people I know are at the mercy of a dealer. They want indica, but Candyman shows up and only has sativa. You're still gonna take it. It's like chicken nuggets instead of chicken tenders. Whatever. Not what you wanted, but you'll take it because he's there and you don't want to think about being not lit for another minute. But if you have the option, I say start with sativa and end with indica. Like starting with a cocktail and have wine with dinner. You don't wanna slam Jäger all night then switch to a Pinot. (See chart for what you may like.)

If you pass someone a pipe or a vape, tell them how to smoke it. Don't make them fumble and ask "Do I press anything?" Yeah, bitch. My right nipple. If someone tries to light a weed pipe from below, do not meth-shame them. Party over here, party over there. It's all the same. Nobody is trying to hurt anyone. I see people do crystal meth in Australia the way I see people do coke over here. It's more social. I've also seen way fewer than twenty-eight to thirty-two teeth per mouth there, so go figure.

If your friends pass out, make sure they're on their stomach so they won't asphyxiate on their own vomit. You're welcome.

In order to have a good time, it's often necessary to give up a part of oneself. I'm not talking about surrendering to the music or any diatribe like that. I'm talking about vomiting. One night, after watching my friend throw up into a plant at a club, she told me, "Sometimes, ya gotta throw up to blow up." She said it helps the roll kick back in when you're partying. I believed her and gave her a mint. If that doesn't help kick-start your **kiki**, sobering up a little might be a good idea. It may even be time to leave the party. Especially if you've taken your shoes off or you've started crying while sitting on the floor of a club. That's the nightlife equivalent of tapping out.

For a smooth exit, hit the head and splash some water on your face. Blow your nose and

literally clear your head. Check for eye boogers. Now, if you think you can keep it together, do a lap around the club, find where the air vent is in the ceiling, and push whatever fat girl is dancing under it outta the way. You can also lunge toward her like you're gonna spew again, but be careful 'cause some people like that (it's called a Roman shower). Either way, the vent is yours now. Feel that refreshing air wash over you. Dance a little

Best Boss Ever. *2015 VMAs.*

on your own. Try to keep the beat so you don't look like you're just wandering around the club, looking for a place to fart. Don't fall, or security will kick you out. It's also why you never wanna throw up in the bathroom unless it's a single hitter. Some asshole will feel the need to come out and act like you're giving birth to a prom toilet baby in there by telling everyone.

Not all subscribe to the "throw up to blow up" theory. If you do get kicked out, make sure you don't yell at anyone. Everyone there is just doing their job. Screaming "Only Jog can gudge me, asshole" will only make you look idiotic and your soberer friends will make fun of you later. Handle your ejection with as much dignity as possible. Even if you have only one shoe 'cause you threw the other one at that bitch who was looking at you weird and that's why you got tossed onto the sidewalk. That's the club's shoe now. You should just go. Losing some footwear is the closest you'll ever get to this being a Cinderella story, though. Remember, there will be more parties and more weekends. If you get bounced, do not try to get back in. At this point, you're what's considered a liability to the club and it's no-can-do. Miley Cyrus said, "Going out doesn't make you a bad person, just like going to church doesn't make you a good one."

I know we all have that one toe that kills by the end of stiletto-wearing night, but never take your shoes off in a club. Aim for 2015 Britney, not 2007 Shitney. Who do you want to be after two a.m.? The bitch who eats shit she wouldn't eat sober? The bitch who stays up till five trying to still have fun and then sleeps till two the next day? The bitch who puts things in her mouth from boys she won't even call when the sun's up? I try to be the person my dog would want me to be. I don't want him to feel bad about pooping inside because Daddy is passed out and can't walk him. Even if I'm still in the outfit from the night before, I'm gonna do my duty so he doesn't do his doodie in the house.

L to R: A dirty dog and their pet Warner.

YOU MIGHT HAVE A PROBLEM IF...

I was struck by a drunk driver on the sidewalk while bike riding when I was thirteen years old. Drinking and driving is terrible. That's why I only drive stoned. If you want to get twisted at a party, I encourage you to smoke pot and not drink. You should never plan on getting pulled over, but if you are, an officer can check your blood alcohol level instantly with his little blow-buddy machine. There is no machine like that for pot. Always insist on a urine test if you're pulled over, because that cannot be administered in the field and lots of times the cops don't want the hassle of risking a time lapse and you pissing clean. I think everyone who's smoked pot will agree that it's a different kinda altering substance than booze. Driving stoned and driving drunk are probably both bad. But I know I'd rather be smoky than sloshed if I had to choose between the two while driving a van full of nuns or something. I'm a terrible driver, but I make up for it with aggressive tendencies. I'm also negligent as fuck when I drive as is. Turning my head constantly to check mirrors always rats up my wig in the shoulder/neck area, so I usually just speed up instead of checking my blind spot. With pot, I'm paranoid as fuck that I'm gonna be arrested, so I'm smart enough to wear a shorter wig.

The other good thing about marijuana is that you can't overdose. Not that it's a goal or anything. I've never OD'd or blacked out, but I also had my first drink at six. My grandmom owned a bar and rationalized letting me try blackberry brandy because she thought it had fruit in it. By nine I knew I hated vodka, and by ten I knew why Malibu Barbie was so happy: it was all the coconut rum the dumb slut drank.

Not many can go as hard as a drag queen, so don't judge those who might need a quick ER trip. Overdosing in your twenties is fine. Everybody gets one free OD. But if you do it in your thirties, you're not doing that right. You know damn well by then that your party should never impede your social life to a degree that there are sirens louder than whatever everyone is trying to jam to. We've all had those times when a three-day weekend turns into a five-day tweakend. At some point, you'll be like "Why is Judge Judy airing on a Sunday?" and then you'll realize it's actually Tuesday and you definitely missed your brunch plans. This is when you'll wanna empty the ashtrays, open the windows, and breathe some new life into your brain...especially if any of the following ever made ya go "Hmmmm...":

• If you know that baking powder must be substituted for baking soda in combination with crack cocaine, plus 1 teaspoon of water

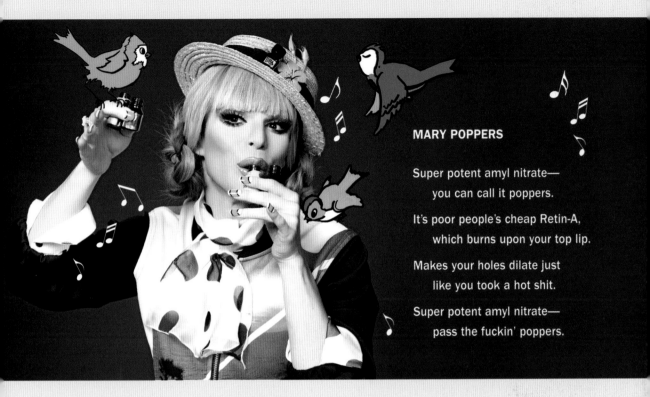

MARY POPPERS

Super potent amyl nitrate—
you can call it poppers.

It's poor people's cheap Retin-A,
which burns upon your top lip.

Makes your holes dilate just
like you took a hot shit.

Super potent amyl nitrate—
pass the fuckin' poppers.

when cooking in high-altitude climates, you might need to Google "in-patient recovery." If you have to, set a timer for your dosages in order to have a good time.

• If your porn tastes are veering into the more extreme subcategories, like suffocation, sounding, fisting, transsexual donkey adventures, cake farts, or anything else so far from the beaten path that even guys from Berlin pass, you may wanna explore what has pushed you in those directions. Amphetamines (e.g., tina, coke, Adderall) affect your brain's ability to get turned on.

It sometimes makes it harder for you to get into the mood without pushing boundaries further than you would without them. A totally straight high school friend of mine got really into transsexual porn once he got into crystal meth. (I know this because he Facebooked me after ten years of nothing, asking if I "partied" and if I was coming back to my hometown for Christmas. I recognized immediately that his motivation was to get some dirt in my skirt and I gave him a hard pass/soft maybe.) Another friend ruined his sex life and several duvets with his

175

Despite what was written in the classic song "Blurred Bynes," you can smoke a Glade PlugIn. Never did I witness Amanda Bynes doing so, though. She walked in on my pissing once at a friend's BBQ and was sketch as fuck. (Hi, Bert and Clay!)

popper use. He couldn't get off without them and just stopped having sex without them. He also liked to inform people rather loudly that it wasn't herpes on his lip, it was just a poppers burn. It actually resurfaces your skin like a peel if it comes in contact too fiercely.

- *If you're ever worried about having to piss clean, you pretty much have a problem. You should be able to stop whenever you want. Otherwise, it's officially something you should get a pamphlet for. Don't try to Google "shotgunning marijuana through*

your ears" because you think you can get high without it showing up on a drug test. It doesn't work. Britney didn't shave her head just because she had split ends. She shaved her head because she probably thought she was gonna lose custody of her kids if they drug tested her with a hair strand test. It's gonna show up.

- *If you're at the dentist and you ask for a few more minutes on the nitrous just to "relax," you need to get your parking validated and go. It's not a day spa for you and your good-time*

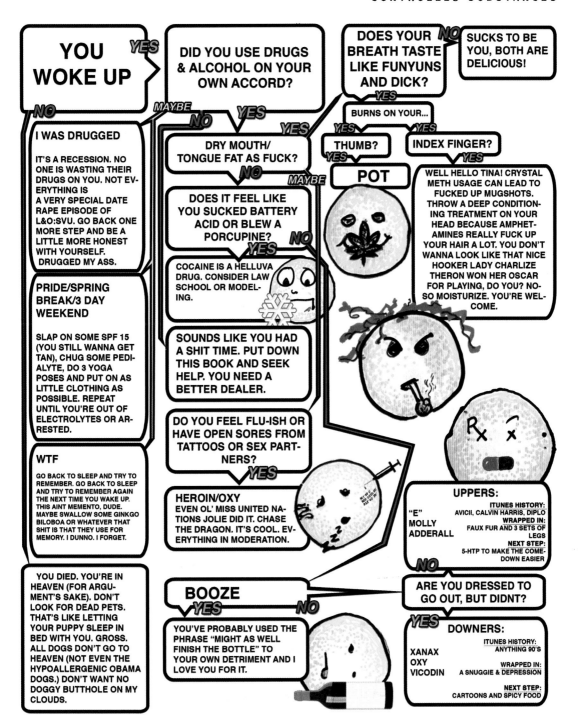

YOU WOKE UP

YES

DID YOU USE DRUGS & ALCOHOL ON YOUR OWN ACCORD?

DOES YOUR BREATH TASTE LIKE FUNYUNS AND DICK?

NO

SUCKS TO BE YOU, BOTH ARE DELICIOUS!

NO

MAYBE

NO

YES

YES

BURNS ON YOUR...

YES

YES

I WAS DRUGGED

IT'S A RECESSION. NO ONE IS WASTING THEIR DRUGS ON YOU. NOT EVERYTHING IS A VERY SPECIAL DATE RAPE EPISODE OF L&O:SVU. GO BACK ONE MORE STEP AND BE A LITTLE MORE HONEST WITH YOURSELF. DRUGGED MY ASS.

DRY MOUTH/ TONGUE FAT AS FUCK?

NO

MAYBE

THUMB?

YES

INDEX FINGER?

YES

POT

WELL HELLO TINA! CRYSTAL METH USAGE CAN LEAD TO FUCKED UP MUGSHOTS. THROW A DEEP CONDITIONING TREATMENT ON YOUR HEAD BECAUSE AMPHETAMINES REALLY FUCK UP YOUR HAIR A LOT. YOU DON'T WANNA LOOK LIKE THAT NICE HOOKER LADY CHARLIZE THERON WON HER OSCAR FOR PLAYING, DO YOU? NO SO MOISTURIZE. YOU'RE WELCOME.

DOES IT FEEL LIKE YOU SUCKED BATTERY ACID OR BLEW A PORCUPINE?

YES

NO

COCAINE IS A HELLUVA DRUG. CONSIDER LAW SCHOOL OR MODELING.

PRIDE/SPRING BREAK/3 DAY WEEKEND

SLAP ON SOME SPF 15 (YOU STILL WANNA GET TAN), CHUG SOME PEDIALYTE, DO 3 YOGA POSES AND PUT ON AS LITTLE CLOTHING AS POSSIBLE. REPEAT UNTIL YOU'RE OUT OF ELECTROLYTES OR ARRESTED.

SOUNDS LIKE YOU HAD A SHIT TIME. PUT DOWN THIS BOOK AND SEEK HELP. YOU NEED A BETTER DEALER.

WTF

GO BACK TO SLEEP AND TRY TO REMEMBER. GO BACK TO SLEEP AND TRY TO REMEMBER AGAIN THE NEXT TIME YOU WAKE UP. THIS AINT MEMENTO, DUDE. MAYBE SWALLOW SOME GINKGO BILOBOA OR WHATEVER THAT SHIT IS THAT THEY USE FOR MEMORY. I DUNNO. I FORGET.

DO YOU FEEL FLU-ISH OR HAVE OPEN SORES FROM TATTOOS OR SEX PARTNERS?

YES

UPPERS:

"E"
MOLLY
ADDERALL

ITUNES HISTORY:
AVICII, CALVIN HARRIS, DIPLO
WRAPPED IN:
FAUX FUR AND 3 SETS OF LEGS
NEXT STEP:
5-HTP TO MAKE THE COMEDOWN EASIER

HEROIN/OXY
EVEN OL' MISS UNITED NATIONS JOLIE DID IT. CHASE THE DRAGON. IT'S COOL. EVERYTHING IN MODERATION.

YOU DIED. YOU'RE IN HEAVEN (FOR ARGUMENT'S SAKE). DON'T LOOK FOR DEAD PETS. THAT'S LIKE LETTING YOUR PUPPY SLEEP IN BED WITH YOU. GROSS. ALL DOGS DON'T GO TO HEAVEN (NOT EVEN THE HYPOALLERGENIC OBAMA DOGS.) DON'T WANT NO DOGGY BUTTHOLE ON MY CLOUDS.

BOOZE

YES

NO

YOU'VE PROBABLY USED THE PHRASE "MIGHT AS WELL FINISH THE BOTTLE" TO YOUR OWN DETRIMENT AND I LOVE YOU FOR IT.

NO

ARE YOU DRESSED TO GO OUT, BUT DIDNT?

YES

DOWNERS:

XANAX
OXY
VICODIN

ITUNES HISTORY:
ANYTHING 90'S
WRAPPED IN:
A SNUGGIE & DEPRESSION
NEXT STEP:
CARTOONS AND SPICY FOOD

gums. It'll also make your dental hygienist look at you judgey as fuck. *(Hi, Deann!)*

- *If you ever say you're gonna "do some Motrin" or "do an Adderall," you have a problem. You take medicine and you do drugs. #Duh.*

- *If you're ever wondering if there's a recreational level of carbon monoxide use just to try it, you should move to someplace with just a carport. There is no "recreational level" of carbon monoxide use. There's either "not at all" or "suicide."*

- *If your BF is your weed dealer, and you start dating him and stop giving him money, that kinda makes you his crackwhore. Pussy market value usually doesn't outweigh pharmaceutical needs, be they recreational or necessary.*

- *If you've ever found yourself in a relationship with someone who supplies you with drugs and you still pay him, well, then you're a crackwhore with a side of stupid. If either of you breaks up with the other, **debtiquette** dictates that you must at least offer to start paying for ass or grass, respectively. Don't try calling your dealer at eleven p.m. Make a plan early and stick to it, preferably while the sun is up. You don't wanna start pre-partying with an **RBV** and then have your friends*

show up with a bottle of G or something incompatible like that.

If this interventional page didn't work, and you go to jail, sorryboutit. I tried. I've been inside and it was not fun. I didn't mind the cavity search, but there is nothing to do. I came to the conclusion that cops are mean sometimes because they have to wear super ugly, unflattering uniforms, which makes them act out on others and fuck up minorities. I was alone my whole time there in the LGBT section, other than this one cellmate for, like, eighteen hours who took the loudest dump in front of me, ruining my Oz Christopher Meloni fantasy. I stacked up the four bunk mattresses in my cell and had a nice "Princess and the Pea" fantasy nap. I could hear the music from the club across the street from the sheriff's station in WeHo. I distinctly remember them playing "Stranger in my House," 'cause who doesn't love Tamia and plus irony. My other legal suggestion (and this is from my LA Lawdog man) is this: if you ever have to take a lie detector test, act like you have a cold and sneeze and sniffle a lot. It throws off the bearings and makes the measurements tweak more than the walking-on-sunshine girl from Intervention.

How to **SUCK LESS** at

ENTERTAINTING

COMPANY PICNIC

I love going out. I got my first fake ID when I was sixteen by standing in a college park in West Philly and offering any white blond people I saw two hundred dollars for their ID. I found one within an hour and gave him my full name, address, and home phone number because I wanted him to be sure I wasn't trying to steal his identity or anything. I just wanted to fuckin' party. And party I did.*

I got fired from my dinner theater job because I threw a plate of spaghetti and called a woman a cunt, mainly because I was wickedly hungover and I snapped when she called me a "rude little fag." I said it was improv, but either way, after that I decided to never let a stupid job stand in the way of my going out. So I started to work in clubs.

Clubs are a stable line of work for unstable people. People without custody of their kids, people who've been in recovery. People who can't find time to get their roots done or their weaves tight-

ened 'cause they sleep all day during regular people hours. Vampires. People who smoke menthols. People who substitute work friends for friend friends. People who figured they'd be at the club anyway so why not get paid to go (that last one was me). I started managing strippers in West Hollywood when I was nineteen, founding a stripper booking agency called Boxmeat and performing in drag at the same age. Along the way, I've seen lots of piss-poor behavior (a lot of it in mirrors).

It was always my goal to run away and join a circus as a kid, and I now feel like I did just that. It's not only because I find myself under a big top in a new city each night but because I've literally done every job at a club. I've handed out popcorn at leather parties and I was a closing performer at the Life Ball in Vienna for fifty thousand people while singing a song I wrote about buttfucking. These are bible truths from an international glambassador. I mean just look at the pictures. Does

---

* If you wanna get into a club underage, go for it, but don't expect me to help or sneak you in, thus risking my employment. Get an ID or fuck a security guy. (Hey, Big John.) I also won't stand outside on the lookout for you to walk you in. Try a Craigslist ad, like "Hey. I'm underage and really, really wanna party. I'm not gonna steal your mail and don't give a fuck about your social security number. I just wanna see bands I like and buy beer. Don't tag me or tell my mom. I'll give you $250." It'll get flagged, so remember to post it a few times a day in sections that people who need money will frequent (e.g., Rooms Shared, Missed Connections, For Sale). I have a lot of kids trying to meet me at my gigs, where they can't get into the party, and it can be very hit or miss. Beforehand, it's all right, but sometimes these teens wait until the end, and that's just no spot for a kid. I don't need them peeking around the alley, seeing me smoking in the fire exit or looking for a lost earring in the backseat of a car with a new friend.

this look like someone who's dying on the inside? Nope!

Every time I'm onstage, I think of it as a chance to make a ton of new friends. Especially if I have a mic in my hand. It's my job to keep the night going at a pace that everyone can enjoy, whether they've got alcoholic atrophy or coke jitters. It's the entertainer's job to always put a positive spin on things, even when something sucks. Energy up and attitude down. If some shit happens, just wipe it up and flush it. Sure, you can mention the pink elephant shit in the room, but talking shit is not how you make friends, and that's what you want really…friends, right?

Errant testicle meat is often described as bubblegum because it looks like smashed Bazooka Joe on a sidewalk and it's been in people's mouths at some point.

Friends who give you money. In business school they call it "marketing," I bet. I dunno. I didn't go to business school. I hear they also teach you to find a niche and fill it. No one was managing strippers in LA before I opened Boxmeat, so I basically checked that off niche-wise, and now I can get my niche filled in return as easy as one text, two text, three text, whore.

Tipping is a *huge* part of nightlife. It helps you get treated in a manner better than those who don't tip. When people tip a stripper, bartender, performer, or bouncer, they're not tipping for their health. They're tipping to buy someone's undivided attention for a split second, whether it's to lightly graze a taint with a dollar or to communicate "There's more where that came from" to a security guard to overlook the giant line and let you in. Time is money and rarely is it unwelcome. Wait. I forgot about mouth money. If I get sick at a club, I want it to be from making

out with a stranger and not from putting your dirty five-dollar oral offering into my mouth. Upon examination, the two things most found on money are cocaine and feces.

If there's a show going on, it's not the best idea to interrupt a performance unless there's money in your hand. If you know a song, sing along. But don't get crazy. I mean look at what happened to that other kid from *Glee*, right? If you do interrupt a performer, it's best to be

Speaking of huge chunks of flesh flying through the air, it's always a good idea to make sure you know you'll be caught when stage diving. Sometimes people would rather keep their drink than hoist a hog body.

prepared for anything. I've seen big girls use their bodies as weapons onstage to physically hurt people by *Operation Dumbo Drop*ping some punk for pulling focus.

Don't fuck with a stripper either, because they have a way of marking the bad tippers. A simple hug from behind will leave glitter or makeup all up the back of a man's shirt, so he doesn't know it but his girl at home sure will when she cleans it. It's called "booty dusting." Getting got by the game is just the way it goes. Not every performer is a single mother trying to get back custody of her kids. I mean what would you do if your son was at home, crying all over the bedroom floor 'cause he's hungry—and the only way to feed him is to sleep with a man for a little bit of money? I would go to cosmetology school while working nights and maybe not go ass to ass with a girl named Diamond at a junior high friend's apartment.

That being said, a performer should never expect an audience to tip. It's kinda looked at as a given in America and that's a shame. Nothing wrong with a **park and bark** number if you're certain the audience is gonna worship you for your looks, but don't try it if you're just gonna do the bare minimum. It can even be artful because, again, a lot of audience members want to have their favorite porn star's or drag queen's attention

These nice people literally pulled off my fake nails as keepsakes in Rio.

for that one second and a brief skin-on-skin dollar exchange. Standing at the edge of the stage with a tip bucket while lip-synching will earn you the nickname Smoke Break from me. It's twofold too, because not only does it make you look like a lazy, emphysema-ridden stage clog but you're also the reason people go outside to get cancer. Speaking of illnesses, I saw one aggressive performer yell, "The big bills have AIDS! Gimme all your twenties and save yourself. I'll be your warrior." This was in San Francisco—not exactly the place to make HIV jokes. Knowing your audience is key. If people ain't tipping, maybe suggestively do your next number with a follow spot while sitting on an ATM. At a drag queen convention in LA, with tickets sixty dollars and up, many drag queens charge for photos, and I think that's tacky as fuck. It's like going to Disneyland and having Mickey Mouse ask for some scratch before you pose with him. I'd rather make money off my talents than my time. No **Rupaulogies**.

If you get an inch, don't try to take a mile. I'm not super into tons of hugging and I never really kiss anyone. For one, you'll just end up eating my wig. When a drag queen or girl does her hair, she doesn't usually think "Gee, I hope I get to restyle my hair with about fifty people's sweaty faces." Smooching everyone who tips is about as smart as drinking out of a needle exchange container. F'real. If I get sick, I can't sing and do my job. So back up outta my bubble with the stranger danger.

How about a nice fist bump or a half hug so

your arms don't move the wig I glued to my temples? Just slip a hand around my waist and grab my ass bowling-ball style. Slip a finger in for balance and blame it on vertigo. Same thing with a stripper. Not everyone can make the clown spit, so stop tugging on his dick like you're gonna get a prize. If a performer leaves the stage, do not bum-rush them like a fraternity party rape circle. I personally invite all gratis forms of contact, provided there is no fluid exchange (ask Katya). If you want a picture, leading with a tip is optional but a flash is not. Turn that flash on and be ready to go. Never trust the auto on your phone. Auto is a bitch. Flashes are great because it's easier to filter something down than lighten it up. Take your damn phone case off, too. You know it makes shit crazy like an eclipse. You may only get one shot. Don't come back at me saying "Oh no, it's blurry." You say blurry, but I say pre-filtered. If the occasion to take a picture arises at an organized kinda step-and-repeat gig, don't ask for a selfie. The promoter will say no because they make their money selling as many people as quickly as possible. It's easier to say "Sorry" than "May I?" Just run-and-gun that picture and selfie the fuck outta it. Again, make sure the flash is on! I'm a man and you're probably drunk.

That being said, try to have it, like, 50 percent together when meeting the person you came out to see. Don't throw an arm up around your idol if you're sweaty and your pit stinks. I don't wanna smell like your BO the rest of the night unless we're fucking. Once in the UK, a man's breath smelled remarkably like a combination of egg salad and ass. Like he maybe fed his asshole an egg salad sandwich and then it crawled up to his face so he could breathe it into my air space. There's always the one dumbass who thinks it's OK to shit at the club. Believe me. The stalls are not for pooping. Think of them as vice chambers. Do your drugs in there or suck dick, but don't fuckin' poop. That's nasty. Go to McDonald's and buy something off the dollar menu so you can get a bathroom token to blow their spot up. I'm trying to dance and do not need to smell your ass wafting in from the men's room. Oh, this is a good time to give a shout out to all the idiots in the club wearing flip-flops who like to get irate with me when I step on their toes, like I do it on purpose. You're dumb.

While we're on the subject of piss, one of the best things you can do ever is go up to a performer and say, "Here is a hundred dollars. Piss yourself onstage." Rip the bill in half and give them one half. If they actually do it, it's one of the funniest things to watch, and you can give them the other half. I've only done this once, in a Dallas strip club. Nothing like making someone piss themselves on a warm summer night to really remind you of the reason you started going out.

I started doing drag not just to have fistfights with drunk people but to also find my tribe. Us drag queens, porn stars, go-go boys, transsexuals, and the dykes working the door were always the ones who weren't respected by the higher-ups in the LGBT world. One of the first activism groups, the Mattachine Society, in the '50s and '60s rejected any participants who weren't clean-cut and white. Hell, even Logo TV, when they started, didn't want anything to do with drag queens (I know because I was on two pilots that were flat-out rejected due to drag presence being shunned). I love going to drag shows, not just to see the shows but to go backstage and talk to the other performers. And when an entertainer is onstage, you can go through their bags in the back and really get to know them.

The varied crew of show people aren't the popular kids—we're more like the ones who had detention together—but we're always the first on the scene to help when there's a fund-raiser or a barrier that needs to be broken down. I consider myself a slacktivist and, while we're at it, an **intactivist**. I get shit done my own way. So many visible performers (mostly porn, other than me) being on PrEP and openly talking about HIV has made it less of a stigma for people to feel OK protecting themselves against it. We are not all part of that one mess they show on the news during Pride each year. We are entertainers, and our job is the best job in the world. If you're a performer and you're reading this, I super-duper salute you. You make people happy, whether it be by being the closest thing to Beyoncé they'll ever get to see lip-synch live or by helping them stroke one out during your jerk-at-work bathhouse matinee show gig. Seriously. Good job. Now go wash your hands, 'cause I don't want your herpes on my book.

HOW TO GET PEOPLE TO MOVE IN CROWDS:

■ *Bend over and make retching sounds while splashing ankles with drinks.*

■ *Put two fingers on the fat roll flank area of whoever is in your way and apply pressure. Shifting their center of gravity will make at least one foot move.*

■ *Try **cupcaking** a fart up to them and then loudly say, "Whoever is busting ass is nasty," and proceed to push through like you're outta there.*

How to **SUCK LESS** at **YOUR CAREER**

Finding out what you're good at and then figuring out how to get paid to do it is the easiest way to a solvent and happy future. (I took that from a magazine with Oprah on the cover). "Solvent" means you have money not from credit card advances or your parents. The proper job will allow you growth while at the same time self-discovery. That sounds right, right? Again, my only real job as an adult was dinner theater, and I was fired from that for aggressive improvs. I might've been wrong, but I was too drunk to remember so I didn't think apologizing would be appropriate. Plus, I was eighteen at the time, so it was their fault I was drunk in the first place kinda. I couldn't have begun to properly apologize because I didn't know *why* I was sorry.

Just saying sorry is for suckers—ya have to relay why you're sorry or how you'll avoid doing it again. But saying you "made a mistake" could be a potential get-out-of-jail-free card. It's short and it basically apologizes for you without saying sorry. Using the S word indicates feelings, and everyone knows emotions are for ugly people. "Sorry" reeks of weakness and assigns all the blame to you instead of summing it up to the other variables that may have been involved. So use that GOOJF card carefully, because if you repeatedly

cop to a mistake, it's no longer a mistake. It's a decision. Insanity is defined as repeating the same behavior and expecting different results. Standing behind your decisions, successful or not, is always respectable, so don't ever half-ass anything. Use your full ass or nothing.

Sometimes you just gotta keep your head down, keep your nose clean, and do the gig. Be an asset in any task you're given and they won't care if you don't shit rainbows. Look at Vanna White. She was made obsolete as soon as the letters went digital, but she flew under the radar and didn't make any noise. Smiled pretty and walked over to that vowel that homeboy just bought. The hair was always right, she stayed outta the tabloids, and she was the perfect example of how to keep a job. She even laughs at that jack-off Pat Sajak's jokes. He should be every man's example of what not to do, because hair color on men is never the look. Pat, I'd like to solve the puzzle. What is "Please have several seats."

Sajak probably went to a few of that old closet case Merv Griffin's all-male pool parties and signed a lifetime deal, but Vanna might've just let the right network exec finger her. Women are

If you can't be the sharpest tool in the shed, be a ho #FFA.

BOXMEAT, Inc.
(323) 863-3354

| weho | ca | e: noextrai@aol.com | f: strippers don't fax

lucky because vaginas have so much power. They can give life, they can make noises, they can commit blackmail. That's why I'm of the school that if you have a vagina and your boss wants to play Guess How Many Fingers I'm Holding Up in It, you should go for it. Bossman can, like, never terminate you 'cause he will always worry you'll sue or tell the nice lady whose picture is on his desk. So trust me. Let him finger you. It's money in the bank, girl. I let someone almost make me into a hand puppet at this one gig where coworkers aren't supposed to fraternize, and it STILL besmirches the fags who couldn't keep it under wraps.

I personally ran a much tighter business, and not just because assholes are invariably tighter than vaginas. More than a few strippers, many will not be shocked to learn, are accustomed to using their looks and sex in exchange for goods or services. They may have thought that allowing me to be their casual sperm repository would merit them better or more shifts, but if they ever asked, I always wiped my mouth and told them, "No way, José" (his stage name was Angel, though).

I know there's an old phrase that says that when you assume, you make an ass out of you and me, but I think it mostly makes an ass outta whoever does the assuming. I considered myself more of a one-man volunteer effort, helping underprivileged children by swallowing them before they are born. The couple of times when I may have done some things that were less than California-workplace code-compliant, it showed

me that respect for the pecking order is always a hefty thing to gamble. Somewhere in the middle of Boxmeat's fourteen-year run, I was being paid by twenty different clubs in SoCal to staff their go-go dancers. I had over one hundred people working for me. I loved it. It enabled me to be around the beautiful people, in the middle of a circle where a weird, funny kid like me could have previously only participated from the periphery. I still have a stake in the company and will never give it up. The Eagle could call and say so-and-so's ass is dirty, and I would go right down, rip them off the box, and give them a good scolding. Wait. Never mind. They love that BO in Silver Lake.

Being the boss wasn't always an easy thing. Even though it's much harder to fuck someone over to their face than on the phone, I always treated the people who worked for me how I wanted to be treated, and that meant delivering bad news face-to-face. If someone was fat or cracked out, I would go to wherever they were slinging it that night and pull up a picture on my phone of what they'd looked like when I hired them. Asking point-blank if they thought they still looked like that would usually be a wake-up call. I would always let them dance for tips or turn tricks in the handicapped stall shittercritter style until they were back in shape.

Those who say that failure isn't an option are super wrong. It's actually the easiest and most popular one. You think I'm joking but I'm not. Like, I'm actually not a funny person. I'm just a dickhead and people think I'm kidding a lot. Some might only laugh because the only other option is to cry. Crying at work is the biggest *no* of all time. Unless you just got your hair or your balls or your ball hair caught in a paper shredder, you better never cry at work. Feelings have no place in the workplace.

Complaining that someone hurt you or made you feel bad is crap. You feel how you feel because you're the only one controlling you. If you're treating someone poorly, it's more of a reflection of whatever you're going through than how you actually feel about the person. There's no justifying it. Not even with some lame horoscope shit. Using the zodiac or planets to justify behavior is the worst! Mercury does not retrograde directly up anyone's ass. Like, IDGAF if you're a Gemini. I hate both of you! If you ever get fired, make sure to do your best *Working Girl* scorned bit. Get

If you're late and need to summon tears to keep that gig, suck on a Halls menthol cough drop and then run it along the waterline of your eyeball near your lower lashes. It'll make you start to swell right up like your dog died at your Pop-Pop's funeral. You're welcome.

your stuff, fix your hair, and say the following: "Look, you. Maybe you've got everyone around here fooled with this saint act you have going, but do not ever speak to me again like we don't know what happened. You got me? Now get your bony ass out of my sight." (Substitute "fat" for "bony" if applicable.)

My main job is to entertain, and in that field, it's best to focus only on the people who love you. The haters in no way affect the money. You don't need everyone to support you. If 50 percent of the people hate you and 50 percent love you, that's fine. As far as the revenue stream is concerned, being hated is exactly the same as being ignored. It doesn't make things worse. If someone calls me a cunt at one of my shows over the weekend and it's sticking in my brain on Monday and Tuesday, and then Wednesday, Thursday, Friday is a literal WTF, I might examine why it got under my skin. Maybe I needed a reality check or they didn't like my outfit. Who knows? Every criticism is an opportunity to improve, even if that only includes how you handle it. At least it's said to your face. Don't worry about people who talk about you behind your back. They're behind you for a reason. Try farting.

SUCK LESS SUPPLEMENT

know the previous section applies to very few readers, but if doing what you love also feeds you, that's a key component to making life suck less. I never complain about my job. It's the best ever because I enjoy it even when I can't feel my pinkie toe from some Loubs that are too high. The way I figure it, we're all gonna bust our asses at some point, so it's best to make it something tolerable. I wanted to be a clown, growing up, but that changed once I grasped that my allergies just wouldn't do well around all that hay and carnie folk. I've never actually had a real boss for longer than a month or two as a teen, but I did learn a few real-world workforce tips.

■ If you have a great idea at work but run up against resistance, it might be in the way you're presenting it. Try a little dress rehearsal. Tell your best friend your idea while recording it on your phone. Then listen to it while transcribing what you said, and voilà—perfect pitch to your boss. Also, always try to get the pitch in before eleven or after two. If it goes poorly, at least you know if was your fault and not because they were wondering where the fuck their lunch order was.

■ Don't ever use profanity if things don't go your way at the job. Cursing basically says the point you're trying to make isn't solid enough to stand on its own merit, without swearing. Raising your voice does the same thing.

■ Interrupting is the worst! It's basically saying that whatever the interrupter is saying is more important than whatever the interruptee is spewing. If you get called out for interrupting someone during an argument, it makes you look like an unsportsmanlike player and weakens whatever you're saying. Think about it, let whoever finish saying whatever shit they're spewing, then *strike*!

■ You can't say "anxious" without "shits." Being nervous will make you sound shitty. Take a few deep breaths and keep your shoulders down. People mostly want you to succeed, so there's no reason to bring potential failure baggage to the table.

■ Before I release a video on the Internet, I don't get nervous. I get excited. I plan on people liking it. Drag queens usually make a living out of impersonating other women, but I've made a career outta just being myself. Many of the most successful queens are just themselves, if you look at the contemporaries in my field. I mean I tip my wig to Chad Michaels because not only does he turn out *the* Cher to end all Chers but he has got a catalog of other spot-on characters, like Marilyn Manson and the Mad Hatter. He puts hard work into being the best at what he does, just like I put a lot of hard stuff into me, too. Some of that hard stuff helps to make me the best professional stunt-queen that there is. The most successful people of my kind are entertainers who don't try to push through a catchphrase or have a different personality

online. It's called YouTube for a reason, not SomebodyelseTube. So be yourself. Because if people like a put-upon version of you, you're painting yourself into a corner for a lot of hard work, acting like that same version of you for the rest of your life. Jinkx Monsoon told me she is exhausted at the end of a meet-and-greet because she has to be Jinkxie for each and every person in line wanting to meet this great character she created. I'm super glad I don't have the same problem. If you gotta dress up like Lady Gaga or Rihanna to make some coins 'cause the audience lives for their songs, go for it. Just don't lose yourself under someone else's wiggotry and face chart. What I'm saying is, just root for the home team (you) and let loose. If you find out you sucked, at least you know how to not repeat that same thing and suck less in the future.

■ If you go into business with friends, plan it out like you won't be friends by the end. Stuff goes wrong. For instance, if someone wants to be paid in cash and they don't want to fill out a W-9 for it 'cause their bank account would get flagged by the IRS, since they've failed to file a tax return in five years, *don't do it*. It's not a no-good-deed-goes-unpunished type of thing. It's just common sense. Taxes are the worst. And, hey, if your old girl group is giving you grief, just start a new one. Move on and grow.

SUCK LESS at STRIPPING:
SO YOU WANNA TAKE YOUR CLOTHES OFF FOR MONEY?

So if after reading all of that, you're thinking you want to take your clothes off for money, please read what follows. If you want to be a drag queen, congratulations. Just watch my tutorials and do the opposite.

To become a go-go dancer or stripper, you'll probably have to audition at a club during club hours. If you have a body so crazy good (one of my dancers screen-tested for Superman) or a dick so huge (Nolan Gerard Funk, Versace model) that it doesn't matter if you can stay on beat, then you'll probably get hired as soon as I see your abs. But my general rule is, if you don't make any money on a weekend night during prime time, you won't be getting hired. If I get you down from the box and you're dollarless, don't ask "When do I start?" Ask "Do you know anyone to fix my gynecomastia?"

I'm totally actually lying. I will hire you if you make no money during your audition if I know you're a hooker or just a run-of-the-mill skankpot who will turn bathroom tricks and keep the customers coming back and happy. But warning: Get the money first, Mary. Tell them panty sniffers

"No cashy, no kissy." Don't let nobody try to get your shape before they hit that ATM. This one time, one of my favorite shittercritters texted me, asking for a shift, saying he was "free this hole weekend," and I just didn't have the heart to tell him he was more right than he knew.

Many get sucked into the life of the dance very quickly, overtanning and supplementing, or even worse, doing a cycle of steroids. G'head and do some HGH (which cuts fat), but the steroids are a gamble. They tend to make you break out, and then if you top it with oil, it's just highlighting the skin issues...or what I call "badvertising."

Being able to handle your scandal is something most people think will be easy at the clubs, whether it be sex, liquor, or drugs. With sex, the trick is not to put out with everyone if you're gay. You want a certain amount of untouchability. Mystery equals money. With liquor, it's one of the easiest ways to gain weight. That and disco fries combined with sleeping late can take you from instant hire to lunch shifts only within a month or two. Drugs are the biggie. Drugs can give you nicknames like Grumpy, Roidy, Stubby, or Blackout Bobby. This queen I know named Bubbles was told she was taking MDMA when in fact someone gave her Viagra and she couldn't tuck for a full night. So many go-go boys have tried to tell me they were roofied, and I've made them sit with me while we scrolled through hours of security footage to see if they actually were. I would tell them, "Listen, it's a recession. No one is wasting their drugs on you. So if we don't find anyone dosing your drink on the cameras and you want to keep your job, you'll be working for a month for tips only." You can guess how that went.

Watching people lie when they don't know that I've heard it all before was always the best. "I was at the hospital" was always followed by "Well, show me your discharge papers." "I was in an accident" was always replied to with "Show me a pic of your car." The lie most often told by a performer is when another performer asks "Does this look good?" When an insecure dancer asks, half the people won't care, half the people will say yes even if it doesn't because it's a competition for the customer's coins, and the other half will steal it if it is actually cute. I know that that's three halves, but this is stripper math. Nobody comes to a club wondering what stylistic choices their favorite dancer is gonna wear. One thing, though: Your shoes are a direct reflection of your genitals.

A penis with a PayPal is a dangerous thing. Never pay for hookers with online money transfers. It's considered wire fraud, which is a federal crime.

Dirty sneakers usually equate to pubes that look like a rough patch of grass by the highway on-ramp. Plus, your feet are at eye level if you're dancing on a bar. Otherwise, all the armbands, leg warmers, sunglasses, and anything not used to enhance your sexual organs are superfluous. If you don't know what "superfluous" means, it's basically a drag queen doing "Freakum Dress" in pants. Beyoncé would never.

How to **SUCK LESS** at
SOCIAL MEDIA

34

ocial media isn't really real. It's a buncha words, pictures, and clips edited to garner attention and ultimately compete with each other for virtual ticks of favor. It's a meal that you can keep eating without ever getting full, and I fuckin' *love* it! Sure, it's shallow, but think about when you go swimming. Shallow end—no diving, bitch. Plus, I'm not trying to get my hair wet right now.

Here are some tips to make the Internet a place where you can find food, fun, or fucks. Don't do all three at once. AppleCare don't cover that.

A. Ask. There are no stupid questions. Only stupid fuckin' people who say that kinda diatribe. Generally, the Internet is a place for ho-hums to act like they're Hercules. If someone comes at you wrong, consider your options and then go with my fail-safe one: replying in an attractive, congenial demeanor to further enrage the aggressor. Sometimes this is with a simple smiley face. Sometimes it's with nothing at all. They want a reaction. People love to play keyboard warrior.

B. Brevity is the soul of wit. Keep it short. Keep it simple. Steal it from someone and use it when you don't have an answer.

C. Complaining is draining. No one ever has signed on to Facebook or anything else to say "Hmmmm... Let's see how I can intentionally depress myself today." Have they? No. They

haven't. That's what the news is for. As someone who has no real job but lives offa people enjoying things I say/do/put in my body, I try to spike everything with humor. Chances are your whiny musings won't be Ellen bait, so if you're also trying to make a living as an entertainer, remember the show must go on.

D. Discrimination. You thought this was gonna be "dick," didn't you? Well, it kinda is. You're a dick if you discriminate. If someone says they're offended by something you typed about their race, creed, gender, or natural abilities, you have two options, which both involve apologies: (1) you can apologize that they feel that way, or (2) you can apologize for failing to see how you're the offending party and refer them to A. Again, nothing wrong with asking. Ignorance is the inability to learn after being repeatedly taught...so ask a bitch to teach you. I had a friend who called herself a Chinegro because her dad was Chinese and her mom was Sudanese. I said it once and my mother slapped the shit outta me. I didn't know I was being racist. I try to steer away from race-related humor even though I've had so much dark dick, I get tested for sickle cell. Oh damn. I just did it again. I also impersonated Precious's mom once for a movie and that ended up on the Internet. The director of the movie justified it by comparing it to the Wayanses doing *White Chicks*, but I was the one that took the heat. I apologized sincerely and moved on. But there's always people who want to wallow in someone else's mistakes online, and it's their prerogative. I know I would rather come in outta the rain and party. Have fun and meet new people. Just don't ask your new friends what they're mixed with. People are not salads. When you ask "Are you halfrican or all black?" people know you're really wondering about the texture of their pubes, and it makes you look like a whore.

E. Emoji! Here are some you'll use after reading this book:

F. First Amendment. Say whatever you want. I say "faggot" because I'm reclaiming it, just like "queer" was reclaimed in the '70s and "dyke" was reclaimed by lesbians with big motorcycles. I feel like any pain anyone else has associated with the word "fag" is none of my business after all the pain I went through getting buttfucked a lot by a Dominican dude when I was fifteen. If the slur applies to you, feel free to say it. If it's slur-adjacent, tread carefully. I don't say "tranny" much because it's a hot-button topic. "Tranny" was originally slang for "transvestite" (a man who dresses in women's clothing), but it's since been misappropriated by the porn industry as a moniker for transgender people (individuals who take active steps to change their gender). But me arguing that is like someone asking Winnie-the-Pooh about fire safety. Sure, he lives up in the Hundred Acre Wood, but he really doesn't give a fuck. Pooh just wanna eat honey and get Eeyore to not be such a fuckin' buzzkill.

G. Ghost, as in ghosting that fucker cold. Someone posts your pic without tagging you? Ghost 'em for a day. Someone asks you a question that they shouldn't put you in a position to answer, like "Will you take me to the airport?" Ghost 'em until they're on that damn plane. Friends don't ask friends to take them to the airport. They know damn well they could get a shuttle. A light ghosting like

that last one requires some finesse, because you have to have zero activity on all your accounts. Otherwise they'll know you've been by your phone and woulda seen their message. So if you post, you're toast.

H. Humblebrag. Holding up a pizza box with your six-pack on display or taking pictures while you're volunteering at a soup kitchen are both good examples of humblebragging. If your body is good enough to show off, go have fun with it while you're still young instead of posting braggadocious pics of yourself. Oh, and if you want to do good, just do the good for goodness's sake or to offset all your kleptomania.

I. Inspirational insipidness. Don't post inspirational quotes just to make it seem like less of a humblebrag. Seriously. My friend's model boyfriend du jour posted something about how nothing in this life is eternal and nothing is without it's [*sic*] fault—literally with faulty grammar—then tagged it #legday because his thighs were out. It's like "*Huh?*"

J. Jizz. It's what's all over the floor around where your laptop is. It's also the name of the best things on the Internet: Jiz, the drug-pushing, sex-pimping, gender-bending version of everyone's favorite '80s cartoon pop star on Sienna D'Enema's YouTube channel, which has overdubbed send-ups of *The Golden Girls*, *Punky Brewster*, and Paula Deen. Also, this book was almost named *Queef on My Tits, Bitch: The Willam Belli Story* because of its creator, Evil Jeff.

K. K. Fuck you, autocorrect. When I write "K," I'm trying to say "OK" but shortened, yet spell-check constantly changes it to "I." Fuckin' A! Or actually ducking A, in this case.

L. Libel is a written form of defamation. Slander is a spoken form of defamation. So if you're trash-talking someone blind who uses voice translation reader software to relay info off the computer, you can be sued for both. Don't fuck with blind people. Deaf people you can clown on, though. They never listen.

M. Miley Cyrus. She is my favorite person online because she gave her album away for free and is using her fame and talents to bring attention to worthy causes, like homeless LGBT youth. She is the future for philanthropy, putting her money where her mouth is when it's not wrapped around a blunt or a microphone.

N. Native American prostitute lady man on *Cops*. Google "excuse my beauty" and know that when he told that officer, "I won't work my looks no more," he sure did mean it.

O. Online slang, like ASL BBW M$4M DTF. Just say it. If you have that little time to actually communicate with another person you're trying to potentially fuck, just light a scented candle and get yourself off alone, you illiterate fuck.

P. Pimp game. Keep your pimp game strong, but don't strong-arm. It's OK to make the little googly eyes on a picture of someone half naked, but don't write "I want to be inside you" or some creepy shit like that. So no flirting 'less we gonna be fucking.

Q. *Queer as Folk.* Find the British version on the Internet and watch the hot blond dude from *Sons of Anarchy* get his ass eaten out like a Choco Taco. The whole series is really good.

R. Reaching. Don't do it. You know when you're reaching. When someone posts a picture of a party and you weren't there, don't post "Wow—looks fun" 'cause then you look like a whiny bitch baby. I don't automatically become a singing telegram just because you saw me on a reality TV show and you tell me it's your birthday. I've had, like, thirty-three of them, and chances are you never got me a cake or a stripper. So **BGB**. Internet validation is just a drop in a bucket deeper than Buffalo Bill's fat-girl well.

S. Sarcasm. Tone is one of the few things that you can't get delivered on the Internet. If someone says something that's crappy and gets called out for it but then throws an "I was being sarcastic" excuse on it, it really makes you wonder. For instance, I was asked what I would do if I was given a "ginormous amount of Skittles." I replied, "Throw them at trans kids," fully knowing that I could be crucified. Make sure when you make a joke with sarcasm that you use a double-blind technique, which protects you either way. 'Cause maybe I was throwing them at trans kids because Skittles are fuckin' delicious and I was trying to share. (See what I did there?)

T. Tagging. My friend @emersoncollins had the most brilliant Halloween costume of 2015. He combined Lil' Kim with Kim Davis. Miss "four million followers" Chrissy Teigen posts his pic up, probably full-well knowing who he is (and I know this because I follow her and got excited when she tweeted that she loved Bravo's *The People's Couch*, a show @emersoncollins stars on). So Miss Girl goes ahead and posts his pic with no tag. I know, right? You know how the Internet works, Chrissy. I mean it's part of the reason you're so popular. So pay it forward, girl. Tag a bitch next time. Especially when people who enjoy your social media are part of what makes you a success. It's like someone passing you a napkin and you sneezing in it, then handing it back.

U. Untagging. Dude, I will untag you so fast if you look like some first-time-in-drag fool in a brown wig and no tits. Don't tag me. Don't say you're inspired by me. Don't tag me in a picture of an empty table with who you want at your fantasy dinner party. I don't eat in front of strangers, bitch. Don't tag me in a shitty picture of me that you full-well know I won't like. I will not only untag you; I will report your ass. I don't acknowledge every single tag that people post about me, because then it sometimes turns into a weird cycle of them tagging to say "OMG Willam liked this," and nobody wants to see their own paper trail. It's like looking at selfies in the club right after you take them. Weird.

V. Vague. Being vague is lame. If you come to social media to vent about a problem instead of dealing directly with whoever your issue is with, you're acting like a neutered junkyard dog. Don't be passive-aggressive and bark for attention, then lick whatever hand comes through the fence and tells you to keep your head up like Tupac, even though you're a punk. If a friend of mine posts "If you stop telling lies about me, I'll stop telling the truth about you," I will pick up the phone just to be sure it isn't about me, even if we ain't talked in a year. My friend Mathu Andersen told me, "Don't cut your nose off to spite your Facebook," and he's right. Didn't make me stop, but it's definitely under advisement.

W. Wisely chosen words are the best kind. Think twice and type once. Consider the Internet a billboard everyone sees as they go down a highway each day. It's very hard to scrub an image off the Internet. Ask Sam Smith. He had a horrible single where he pranced around gayer than Frankie Grande, and it has been erased from the Internet completely by his team and label because it would've destroyed his credibility. (If you have it, send it to me, please!) I was actually almost sued over something I once wrote half jokingly about a game show having unsafe working conditions and criminal staff activities, and supporting crimes against humanity. I didn't choose my words carefully enough. I should have said the show was "influenced," not rigged, and specified that no blood diamonds or human trafficking occurred. I mean how else would it all play out so perfectly with the world's leading Cher impersonator winning an impersonation challenge, a girl with a criminal record winning a jail challenge, me winning a slut challenge, and Phi Phi winning a travel magazine challenge? (That last one may not make sense, but she won the travel challenge because we all wanted her to go the fuck away.)

X. Exes. The Internet is the best spot to keep up with them. Use it to add fuel to the fire that is the fake fantasy life that you're living in your head. You know, the one in which they return to your loving, whoring arms. Hit up their pages quarterly only… just to see if they still have any seasonal garments you may have left at their homes.

Y. YouTube is a wonderful place to entertain, educate, and explore any number of topics. It's a wonderful place and might be the reason you bought this book. YouTube can make you a pop star or just teach you to pop a zit. Find me there at YouTube.com/noextrai and see what's good.

Z. Ain't really shit that starts with Z, so I'll tell you more about the zits I mentioned up in Y.

Reddit.com/r/popping is a great site for anything that has ever made you go "Does this look infected?" with a fervor for nastiness. Dr. Pimple Popper (aka Sandra Lee) on YouTube is this rad little dermatologist doctor lady, and I love watching her dermatological adventures. She's got ingrown hair removal and cyst vids. The cysts are my favorites, 'cause sometimes the whole sac gets pulled out and it's like a baby is being born, except it doesn't cry and it's made of pus.

#. # No more than three **hashtags**. Don't be that #fagwithtags. The following #'s make you look stupid: #instafamous #nofilter #instaawesome #bae #nohomo #yourewelcome #model #gayguys #inkedmen #scruff #fitfam #masc4masc #vinefamous #tagsforlikes #teamfollowback #yolo #nomakeup #cleaneating #squadgoals #tooblessedtobestressed #bodypostitive #setlife #paintedbyfame #whatwouldyoudoifiwasthere #hausofdolezal #onfleek #abs #gaysofinstagram #instafit #instagay #nofomo.

How to **SUCK LESS** at

INSULTING SOMEONE EFFECTIVELY

Throwing shade has gained popularity in the past few years. Many try, but few succeed. Tone is everything. Reading a bitch is one thing. It's direct and you're detailing their flaws for them, plain and simple. But throwing shade implies that the delivery is shady. It usually involves a twist of some sort that isn't caught until the end. It's all in the pitch. Give out candy-coated tones right up until you push 'em in the oven. You can't let the object of your abjection know what you're thinking until the final blow, thereby obtaining the upper hand by Shutting. It. Down.

Example: I hosted karaoke at a bar in LA, and whenever one of my friends who could wail would come in, I would let them skip the line. Alex Newell from *Glee* came in, and so I beelined for him and asked what he wanted to do. He pointed to the stage and said, "That," meaning he was going to do the same song some little twink was trying to do. So the twink ended, and we welcomed Alex to the stage and got to witness some all-encompassing shade. The whole room was like when it's overcast out, but you still need sunglasses. The song was "And I Am Telling You I'm Not Going" from *Dreamgirls*, and the twink just

sat there stone-faced. All Alex had to do was what came naturally.

And naturally queens know shade better than anyone. Especially the old school ones. Alexis Mateo got me with some old-school shade very effectively, with a simple bait and switch. We were rehearsing with Miley Cyrus for the VMAs and had just completed a run-through. We walked back to our positions, and she grabbed my arm and whispered to me, "Get it together, Mama. They're talking about you over there," motioning to production. She put the fear of God into me for a full two seconds before cracking a smile. It was a simple bluff, and I dunno why she did it—maybe she heard me call her Alexis Potato or something— but one thing is certain: I will never fuck with her again. That's old-school shade right there.

Laying a trap for someone is always a great way to make the target feel even more stupid for walking directly under the shade tree. For example, say there's a blond drag queen in the room who maybe needs to be told what's up:

ME: Wow, you look like Charlize Theron.
THEM: OMG, Charlize. You think? Really?
ME: Yeah, in *Monster*.

Confusion works well, but only if there's plausible doubt. Like if you tell someone they're "really book smart but, like, for a Kindle," it's confusing enough to make them think that you're the actual idiot when, in fact, it'll be bugging them all night. Using negative words but in a joyful manner also works for this. If you hate someone while they're performing, go up to them smiling and snapping, with all your body language saying "*Work*," but maybe actually saying something like "You are so rotted! I live!" Either way, you're disruptive and shit-stirring but still not entirely terrible.

MY TOP 4 SHADY QUEEN MOMENTS:

1 *Telling a girl about to go on stage she has a hair stuck in her lash and then ripping it off (make sure her music has already started).*

2 *For brunch gigs only: put two dollars together along with a piece of bacon between the bills and then tip.*

3 *Getting the audience to buy shots for a girl that just can't say no. I watched Detox cross over so hard, she coulda sworn she was working at Ma'amburger Hairy's.*

4 *Walk up to any blond queen and say "Courtney?" or "Alaska?" and then while they turn around and say "I'm not Courtney" or "I'm not AT5000," look them dead in the eye and say "And you never will be."*

How to **SUCK LESS** at **REVENGE**

've done things that would make the devil himself stand up and slow-clap.

I tour with a lot of my outfits in big ziplocks 'cause I don't want my dresses to get damaged by shoes or whatever else I throw into my suitcase. This one time at a club called B-Bob's in Alabama, I wore a black-and-white striped dress onstage, changing afterward into a tipping dress and putting my stage dress into its ziplock in my tote bag. When I got back to my hotel and unpacked my tote bag to repack my suitcase for the plane, I saw the ziplock was filled with red liquid and the dress was fucked. Someone had poured a drink (vodka cran) into my bag and sealed the ziplock right back up. I was really sad because there had been only four people backstage and I thought they were all my friends. I didn't let it bother me long. When I got home, I dip-dyed the dress pink, overlaying the stain, and threw some rhinestones on it. It's been said that necessity breeds invention and that's not a bareback joke. It means new things happen when they have to, and making that dress pink was my way of seeing the world through rose-colored glasses.

Letting go of the anger and hurt that make a person seek revenge is way more productive than actually seeking revenge. Carrying around all those reasons and pains that lead you to want to even out a score is some *Scooby-Doo* shit. Those old dudes trying to get back at the gang at the end *never* seem happy when they get nabbed, that's for sure. Some bathroom reader Buddhism for beginners guide helped me get rid of a lot of the negativity afterward with the following quote: "A flower does not think of competing with the flower next to it. It just blooms." Once I stopped worrying about being better than all the people I've sailed with career-wise, I was able to focus on just being the best me.

I was in a band with Adam Lambert in the early 2000s and knew I'd never sing like him. Bianca Del Rio will never be surpassed by anyone comedy-wise. After halting that back-of-my-mind contest that only me and the Internet muckrakers were playing, I was able to truly excel at what I love: being a stunt queen who makes people laugh through any form possible. I say enter*taint*er because lots of my humor is ass-related: The video for the song I wrote "Boy Is a Bottom" has over twenty million YouTube views; I buttchug onstage while singing Katy Perry–endorsed parodies of Katy Perry songs; and I've fisted someone while singing "I'm Not a Girl, Not Yet a Woman." Discovering that I didn't have to be

the best singer—or the prettiest or the funniest—
was my career turning point and allowed me to be
happy with what I could give the world.

But in the long run, it doesn't matter. Channel
your fuel to achieve so much that any detractor
can't help but see what you're doing. The best
revenge is success. My achievements while cross-
dressing are so much sweeter to me because
making myself a "thing," as self-serving as that
is, has made it easier for others to be themselves.
I'm on billboards in Europe for Magnum Ice
Cream, I had my picture on Sephora shelves
for two years straight, and I repped American
Apparel. Sure, that last one may have gone into
bankruptcy, but I had a number-one album debut
on *Billboard*'s comedy chart at the same time. All
these things (which I list again in my author bio),
braggadoucheus as they are, lead to visibility,
and visibility leads to conversations, and that can
lead to good change. (Bad change is when people
throw quarters at me onstage—Hi, Detox!)

If none of that has helped you realize revenge
is a fool's game, I would just find a way to take a
shit in someone's toilet tank. An upper decker is
like high-fiving someone with shit in your hand.

This is my second-favorite way to see the world:
through rose-colored glasses.

THE BEST WAYS TO GET REVENGE LIST

I was infamously able to keep my cool when another drag queen flipped her wig on me during RuPaul's Drag Race, and I attribute that to thinking twice and speaking once (and knowing where the camera is before striking to kill). I always take a few deep breaths. When you yell and get hyped, your brain doesn't get as much oxygen as it would when you're breathing properly. So deep breaths. You can even use that time to formulate a stealth retaliation. You want a clear path to revenge that will indicate utter defeat in the opposing party compounded with a perplexity as to who or what put the events into motion. The inability to credit a specific person with the blame will let the asshole know "Wow—my behavior sucks enough that it could be any number of people" and hopefully encourage the asshole to change. The anonymity is key. Here are a few ways to fuck with people **boots**.

■ *Send porn to their parents' address in their name. Chances are their mom gets the mail and will be too weirded out to mention it, so it'll just fester her every thought about her son liking piss-party MILF porn or something. And if they do actually address it, chances are the parents won't believe them when they say it's not theirs.*

■ *If you live with someone, take their ice cream and throw it in the microwave for a few seconds— enough to make it slip out like a baby iceberg. Now take a Band-Aid (new or used—your choice), put it at the bottom of the container, and replace that baby iceberg. Throw the carton back into the freezer and live your life.*

■ *Cookie butter. This is the same as above but worse. Scoop cookie butter out of the jar down to the label so from the outside it looks normal. Then put a turd in it (animal or your own). Plop the scooped cookie butter back in while taking care to not disturb the poop too much. The contents on top will be fine. The person won't smell it until after a few uses or they actually eat the stuff that's by the brown-town surprise. This is pretty vulgar, so I don't recommend doing it unless you really are over someone. I mean there are only so many people who will have had access to your cookie butter.*

■ *Slashing tires. Never slash all four wheels! If all four tires on your car are slashed, insurance usually covers it. If it's just one, it's out of pocket.*

■ *Place a used false eyelash in a man's bedroom or car or somewhere his partner will find it. It'll lead the partner to think he's either a cross-dresser on the sly or slipping it to a pole dancer.*

■ *Upper decker is a time-lapse revenge tactic. What you basically do is shit in someone's toilet tank. It will eventually go away on its own, but its torment is a solid ten outta ten.*

The best revenge is looking good. Go check out "Blurred Bynes" on my YouTube channel and see what this dress looked like before the world decided to shit in my purse.

How to **SUCK LESS** at
NOT LETTING PEOPLE KNOW YOU'RE DUMB

37

School can suck. I had a few great teachers, but most of them made me never want to set foot in another classroom again. I didn't go to college because I didn't want to pay to learn stuff I had no clue would be necessary since all I knew was that I wanted to be in *Star* magazine. There are no courses for Who Whored It Better or Gossip. My high school homeroom teacher was such a fuckin' shit starter. She'd always be like "You wanna share that with the whole class?" when I was talking, and I'd be like "No, that's why I fuckin' whispered it, you stupid bitch." Needless to say, I was *done* with school by sixteen. You should quit too, but only if you're sure you're going to be a moderately successful crossdresser who will stumble into a book deal off of

SUCK LESS AT HOOKY

Ya wanna know how to make sure you get sent home from school? Have blood on your shirt in the nippular area. Worked for me twice. The first time I hadn't done my part of a group lab for my third period chem class and didn't wanna tank the group's grade, so I pierced my right nipple in homeroom. The second time I wanted to play hooky 'cause this one dude from an AOL chat room wanted to meet me at the beach for hot-dogging and other lockjaw-related activities. Both piercings were with safety pins and both times were actually behind the areola (I needed the blood effect). It totally worked. It only occasionally shot out puss the next year, but the payoff was other students thought I was officially crazy with a jumbo size helping of street cred. Which is good 'cause high school is like a mental hospital. Do your time and get out as soon as possible. I took an extra optional eighth period one year, satisfied two PE credits with summer school, and managed to leverage volunteering in the office after school into my final elective credit. I took English 4 the summer before my junior year and got the fuck outta high school before I was even supposed to start my senior year at sixteen. There's always a way.

Tumblr (true story). I quit marching band and told my parents that there was no future in learning to make a bumblebee formation on a football field while playing saxophone. I wanted to spend my time in the library learning how to do my own taxes and how credit cards work, and sucking dick in the reference section. You know how hard it is to give a quiet blow job? Now, if I could just get Facebook to stop asking me to finish my profile by completing what university I went to. I didn't go to college; I had gigs.

I was smart enough to figure myself outta the public school system early, but I am not above admitting that homonyms are hard. Differentiating the words that sound the same but are spelled differently will help you avoid douche bags on Grindr or Tinder with so little appeal that they cockblock themselves via spell-check. These little things will make people think you're smarter than you actually are, I bet. If they ask where you went to school, just say an online academy that lets you get your degree at your own pace (you don't need to tell them that your particular pace is super slow and you haven't even gone to the website yet). Fuckin' nosy people. Why are you even talking to them? **BGB**.

"As an escort, I only **accept** money for my time—**except** in this case because your badge is peeking out of your bag, officer," said the lady in pleather.

"Accept" means to receive something, and "except" usually means something other than or aside from whatever.

Your behavior makes me want to say that **you're** an asshole…asshole.

"Your" is possessive and "you're" is a combo of "you" and "are."

Oral sex (**i.e.,** sucking dick) is so much more than just the up-and-down (**e.g.,** breath control, skull fucking, and not vomiting).

"I.e." offers further explanation of something, while "e.g." offers specific examples.

The *principle* that the *principal* is your pal is a **fucktarded** lie
they tell you in school to differentiate the homonyms.

*A "principle" is a fundamental law and a "principal" is usually
something annoying like a school administrator or a loan balance.*

Pep squad sits over *there* because the cheerleaders said *they're* tired
of *their* selfies being ruined by all that talent-free fugliness.

*"There" indicates a location, and "they're" means "they are."
Ownership is indicated by use of "their."*

Whoever *hung* up that stupid "Hang in there" kitten poster
should be *hanged* unless they are hung.

*"Hanged" only refers to the executionartorial act and "hung" is the
past tense/participle of "hang," which means something about a
noose or something that'll fuck you loose.*

It's totally not as big as he says, but it tastes bigger
than when it's in *its* flaccid state.

"It's" means "it is," and "its" is the possessive form of "it."

LEFT & RIGHT

*'m terrible at right and left. I always tell people to make a 'that-way' and point when giving directions.
My little right and left trick is making an L with both hands at the same time and the left hand has the
L going in the correct direction. If you ever have to set a table, remember that both* fork *and* left *have four
letters and* spoon, knife, *and* right *have five.* Fat *has three just in case you're wondering where the dessert
spoon goes.*

DRAGTIONARY

ABC [*ay-bee-see*] slang
"a bitch can't"—when an individual tries despite knowing efforts will be fruitless
Why does Ciara insist on singing live when we know ABC.

acknorigment [*ak-nohr-ij-muhnt*] noun
acknowledgment of something or someone whilst ignoring the same subject
As soon as I saw her fat ass, I gave her a nod of acknorigment to keep her away.

afternoonted [*ahf-tur-noon-ted*] verb
to have had intercourse between the hours of noon and four p.m. with at least one party on a break from work
I got afternoonted real good today and don't want to sit through a long dinner for risk of leakage.

asslete [as-leet] noun
1: an individual who plays games to an inappropriate degree of sportsmanship
2: an individual who plays sports just to show off his body in the respective game's uniform
That asslete in the booty shorts/visible jockstrap combo needs to stop throwing the dodgeball like a ninja assassin.

beat [*beet*] verb or noun
1: (verb) to apply makeup
2: (noun) a makeup job
3: (noun) a place to walk back and forth
After Mathu beat the #AAAGirls faces, they got to the club at last call and then sure did hit that beat from Starbucks to the gay pizza place hard.

Beyoncénically [*bee-ohn-say-nik-lee*] adverb
a way of doing something in a similar fashion to our lord and savior Beyoncé Knowles-Carter
She had tried to do that kick all Beyoncénically, but it ended up looking like she had restless leg syndrome.

BGB [*bee-ghee-bee*] slang
"bye girl bye"
BGB. Hafta poop.

blaccent [*blak-sent*] noun
a manner of speaking that intensifies any type of urban, typically African American twang
RuPaul often uses a blaccent comically, but Tyra's truly came out when she yelled, "We are all rooting for you," at Tiffany.

blaccurate [*blak-yer-it*] adjective
being in the right regarding matters that are African American in nature
Willam's sorry if blaccent offends, but he's totally blaccurate about Ru doing it.

booster [*boo-ster*] noun
somebody who steals to resell for a profit
Call that one booster who got me my living room set to get a six-pack if it's after last call.

boots [*bootz*] grammatical modifier or exclamation (origin: Erica Andrews)
1: (grammatical modifier) a word that adds emphasis to whatever it's used in reference to (a derivative of the phrase "house down boots")
Her behavior at the club was shitty boots.
2: (exclamation) an affirmative response about something that is going to occur
When Mikey said he was coming over for some ass, I was like "Yes! Boots!"

bridealize [*bri-dee-uh-lize*] verb
to go overboard when fantasizing about a
wedding
> *Um, they met on Grindr yesterday and he's*
> *already bridealizing their gay wedding cruise.*

brick [*brik*] noun
a bitch with hard angles and not an ounce of
softness
> *That brick who won the newcomer pageant has*
> *all the softness of a driveway.*

chicken bucket dress [*chik-uhn buhk-it dres*]
noun
a skimpy garment that displays all of one's legs
and breasts like that of a KFC Family Meal and
that one tips around in after the show, aka a
tipping dress or a turnting garment
> *Chaselyn just had her boobs done, so she put on*
> *her tiniest chicken bucket dress even though it*
> *was the dead of winter.*

cliffhanger [*klif-hang-er*] noun
a toe that extends beyond the intended length of
one's shoe
> *These shoes give me a little bit of a cliffhanger*
> *but not full-on Raja foot.*

clock [*klok*] verb
to spot an act or something that is intended to be
stealth
> *Mary, you think you're slick, but I clocked you*
> *trying to steal my tips.*

cubikill [*kyoo-bih-kill*] noun
verbal abuse of a call-in center worker until you
get what you want
> *Initiate a cubikill only when you're certain a call*
> *is not being recorded for posterity.*

cupcaking [*kup-kayk-ing*] verb
the act of farting in one's hand and then
scooping it up toward another individual
> *I told the new shot boy to smell my new Tom*
> *Ford scent, but then I totally cupcaked the fag.*

debtiquette [*det-i-ket*] noun
a standard of ethical behavior one should
subscribe to when in debt to another person
> *Stephen the stripper has owed Willam $600 for*
> *three years but seems to think enjoying vacations*
> *and expensive tattoos is more important than*
> *good debtiquette. Hey girl!*

daywalkers [*day-wah-kuhrz*] plural noun
a term popular for transsexuals and transvestites
who go out in the day but shouldn't
> *Did you see that daywalker run out of the wig*
> *store with her neck looking all gravely and*
> *Nestlé Crunchled?*

dickscretion [*dik-skresh-en*] noun
keeping private matters about private matters
private
> *I won't tell you which X-men's penis I had*
> *in my hand because I have a high level of*
> *dickscretion.*

dickstracted [*dik-strak-tid*] adjective
wasting time on penis-related activities.
> *I bought a Mophie battery case because often*
> *times, I'm too dickstracted to notice my phone*
> *is almost dead.*

disasturbate [*dis-ass-ter-bate*] verb
to flagellate one's genitals with full understanding
that no climax will be reached
> *I continued to disasturbate him, but I knew he*
> *wouldn't be able to cum, being that cocained.*

disrespect [*dis-ri-spekt*] verb (used with an
object)
to render something or someone unreusable, due
to bodily fluids, until suitable maintenance is
given
> *Alaska saw how the trade had disrespected*
> *her sister's new lashes, with his seed rendering*
> *them unreusable.*

DPR [*dee-pee-ahr*] adjective (origin: Detox Icunt) "dick probably right"—a phrase indicating that a gentlemen bystander's penis is of a superlative measurement

Turn around slowly 'cause DPR coming your way in white soccer shorts.

dragamuffin [*drag-uh-muf-in*] noun
an endearing individual with no redeeming qualities visually while dressed in drag

That dragamuffin is a mess, but she always lends me bobby pins, so be nice to her.

dumpster dive [*duhmp-ster dahyv*] noun
the act of going down on anyone who may not be hygienically suitable for activities

Oral sex at Burning Man can sometimes be a real dumpster dive of courage.

fish [*fish*] adjective
when a drag queen looks so passable and feminine that one could imagine his genitals would smell wharf-like, or similar to that of an unwashed vagina

She was so fish, but then she stumbled into a pool of unfortunate lighting and looked like she shoulda been in a Geico ad.

fondude [*fahn-dood*] noun
a man with a cheesy, uncut penis

Tell that go-go boy from Montreal to clean his cock, because we have a no fondude rule in America.

fucktardery [*fuhk-tarrd-er-ee*] noun
asinine or unbelievable behavior

A backstage dressing room is like a locker room and should be free of fucktardery.

furburgering [*fuhr-ber-gher-ing*] verb
to eat hairy pussy

I felt like I was furburgering in a rain forest because her coochie was so warm, wet, and dense.

geish [*geesh*] noun
the state of being in drag

I need to get up in geish real fast for the show, so I'm just gonna do glasses and a lip.

giving me life [*giv-ing mee lahyf*] slang
a phrase indicating that one's actions or intent will yield supreme results

Sonique was giving me life last night with that split out the round-off double back tuck a dick flippy thing she did.

gooked [*gookd*] verb
to get got or to pull the pag

I was expecting a suite with a water view, but the front desk bitch gooked me with this double-bed room by the elevator.

hashtilities [*hash-till-eh-teez*] plural noun
Twitter fights

Hashtilities raged on for a second day as more bar queens shared their frustrations with Willam's propensity for ginking all the bookings.

House in Virginia [*haus in ver-jin-yuh*] slang
"HIV" (also, Apartment in Delaware with Stairs ["AIDS"])

Bitch better use a cumbrella unless you want a House in Virginia.

husbank [*huhz-bangk*] noun
a man whose partner is with him because of his financial status

Bobby is folding shirts at Diesel because his husbank went broke.

insulpliment [*inn-sul-pleh-mint*] noun
an insult crossed with a compliment

Example: Damn. You look so good in that photo I didn't even recognize it was you.

intactivist [*in-tak-tiv-ist*] noun
an individual who is against circumcision

Rhea Litre is a vocal intactivist, mainly because she likes to do body shots out of foreskins.

K

kiki [*kee-kee*] noun or verb (origin: Scissor Sisters—may originate from the proclivity of many revelers to have a key [kilo] of something. Gimme a key…hence kiki.)
a gathering of two or more people while the sun is down
> *We were going to have a kiki at Steven's house, but we couldn't ignore the smell of rotting food from the broken fridge.*

L

L.B.H.P.H.D.W.F.N.S. slang (origin: Krystal Summers)
"long bangs, heavy powder, head down, walk fast, no spook"—detailing possible improvements one could make to better one's chances of not being clocked
> *The only way anyone is ever fucking her is if she gets L.B.H.P.H.D.W.F.N.S., and even then, it'll have to be doggy only.*

M

mop [*mop*] verb (origin: *Paris Is Burning*)
the action of entering a store and just looking… looking for whatever you wanna see…and stealing it* (In general, mopping is stealing. However it's done, it's stealing.)
> *After Carla Extravaganza had her shit mopped, the announcer said, "Will you please return her black patent-leather shoes, size 7? There is a reward. She want her pumps. She said it's not going to work, taking her shoes. Give 'em back."*

mudhoney [*mud-huh-nee*] noun (synonyms: trufflebutter, Santorum, pussy pudding)
a mixture of lube, fluid, and anything else that comes out of an anus from sexual intercourse
> *Some say mudhoney is easily removed from sheets, but I say kill it with fire.*

N

nooch [*nooch*] noun (synonyms: dust, shade, no mind)
nothing, or the state of being ignored
> *Fantasia thought the crowd was gonna live for her, but they didn't give nooch.*

nurse [*nurs*] slang (origin: Jenna Skyy)
a declarative phrase indicating that an individual's look is in need of improvement
> *Ooooh nurse! Your weave looks like a push broom undergoing chemo.*

P

pantysniffer [*pan-tee-snif-er*] noun
an individual of means who provides items and/or support (monetarily or otherwise) to entertaintresses
> *The pantysniffer bought Louboutins and was rewarded with watching his girl sloppily eat a dick dinner.*

park and bark [*pahrk en bahrk*] noun
when a performer stays in the same spot onstage with little movement
> *The girl in the yellow gown knew she was going home because she got a letter from the hotel thanking her for her stay, so she pulled a park and bark during her lip-synch.*

pimptographer [*pimp-tog-ruh-fer*] noun
a person who takes photographs while sexually harassing his subjects or bedding his models (e.g., Terry Richardson [alleged])
> *The agency sent me on a go-see and the pimptographer had an air mattress on the floor.*

pocketbook [*pok-it-buk*] noun
what your momma will hit you with if you don't stop that foolishness
> *Place the money in Detox's pocketbook during her number, but don't look for change.*

---

* For example, walk up to the cash register with the item right under your phone, juggle a few things—another shopping bag, your wallet (have your card out already). If they catch you with the item in your hand, it's easy to play like your hands were just full and you made a mistake…when in fact you're a motherfuckin' stunt queen. If you're too afraid to do that, just shove it into your jail purse. Mall security can't legally make you get naked. (Note, we do not endorse getting caught committing criminal activities.)

pump [*puhmp*] noun
any type of injection or surgical procedure that
thereby plumps the treated area
> *I clocked Miss Brazil's pump at the pag but can't
> tell if it's Juvéderm or 'cone.*

RBF [*ar-bee-eff*] noun
"resting bitch face"
> *Does she have Bell's palsy or is that just RBF?*

RBV [*ar-bee-vee*] noun
"Red Bull and vodka"
> *She said she wanted a sugar-free RBV since she
> was eating French fries.*

residont [*reh-zi-dont*] noun
anything left behind that turns a do into a don't
> *You always think you can scrub off toothpaste
> and semen residue, but it's invariably gonna show
> back up as a residont.*

Rupaulogize [*ruh-pol-uh-jahyz*] verb
a phrase engineered by Willam, later
appropriated by RuPaul, expressing trahnz
apathy
> *Those who say RuPaul should Rupaulogize after
> charging fans at his convention for photos with
> him while he's not even in drag are failing to take
> into account that he doesn't give a fuck.*

saddict [*sadd-ickt*] noun
one who is addicted to sadness
> *That saddict is such a killjoy she'd take the
> funny out of a one-armed girl jumping rope
> with a hot dog. (Hi, Butterscotch!)*

shafterparty [*shahf-ter-pahr-tee*] noun
a party that's turned from a cordial affair into an
"all adult" function
> *Once the last girl left and it was just the guys,
> the kiki turned into a shafterparty.*

shablamgela [*shah-blam-jeh-lah*] verb
to fling oneself on the ground artfully enough
that one is compared to Shangela Laquifa
Wadley
> *The most epic shablamgeling was either Tandi
> Iman Dupree dropping from the ceiling or
> Shangela breaking her leg.*

shimbarrassing [*shim-behr-ah-sing*] adjective
worthy of shame, experienced particularly while
cross-dressing or being especially faggotty
> *It was so shimbarrassing when Courtney's rat
> testicle popped out, but she made it work.*

shipfaced [*ship-fased*] adjective
fucked up on a boat
> *The tequila, sun, and choppy water made Jiggly
> shipfaced.*

shonda [*shohn-duh*] adjective
messy or unkempt, particularly a space where
somebody named Shonda might live
> *I don't know how she even fucks in there 'cause
> her room is so shonda with that litter box in
> the corner.*

sleeptarded [*sleep-tahr-did*] adjective
unable to function after taking too many
downers
> *Paul likes to take a buncha Ambien and then
> get sleeptarded in public.*

southmouth [*sowth-mowth*] noun or verb
1: (noun) vagina or anus
> *That lady's Lululemons are really showcasing
> her southmouth.*
2: (verb) to pay oral attention to someone below
their equator
> *He southmouthed me so hard, his TMJ started
> acting up.*

snatched [*snacht*] adjective
secured rather tightly
> *Miss Thing's ponytail was snatched back as tight as her dick in that swimsuit.*

spermanent [*spur-meh-nehnt*] adjective
existing perpetually and involving sperm (e.g., STIs, pregnancy, stains)
> *If you look under his desk, you can see how spermanent behavior can ruin a nice carpet.*

stenchqueen [*stench-kween*] noun
a stinky drag performer
> *That stenchqueen thinks Febreze and CVS body spray covers the fact that she ain't never wash her drag.*

T, or **tea** [*tee*] noun
1: "truth"
> *She asked what the T was and I told her, "No T, no shade," but she couldn't handle taking T.*
2: testosterone

textual [*teks-choo-uhl*] adjective
sexually inclined, particularly regarding text messages
> *A good way to find out if someone is interested is to send a semi-textual message with an LOL at the end so they can take it seriously or not.*

trade [*trayd*] noun
an individual, usually male, outside of one's sexual grasp who, through circumstances involving money, drugs, or services, renders copulation possible
> *The trade busted in my eye because he knew that I'd hafta go to the bathroom to clean myself up, and that's when he stole my iPad.*

trahnz [*tranz*] noun
a term that encompasses all levels of trans and gender fluidity from first-time-in-drag-at-a-ball and Buffalo Bill to a fully transitioned man or woman
> *That trahnz dodgeball team's secret weapon is all the FTM players on T who are aggro as fuck.*

tranboozled [*tran-boo-zuhld*] verb
when a person has an encounter without revealing their birth gender assignment.
> *I figured my trade knew I was a man but when he asked if I was on the pill, it was clear I had inadvertently tranboozled him.*

transjennerous [*tranz-jen-ner-us*] adjective
(origin: Caitlyn Jenner)
showing a readiness to share showgirl or drag items or be generous with someone who doesn't deserve your generosity
> *The LGBT community was so transjennerous to Caitlyn, but then she went and told Ellen she "wasn't so sure" about gay marriage.*

trude [*trood*] noun
anything that is verifiable fact but also impolite
> *Jade was trude as fuck when she told Alyssa that back fat and halter tops are never the look.*

whorespondent [*hohr-ris-pahn-dehnt*] noun
an anchorperson or correspondent whose slutacious vibe renders all news they report null and strips them of credibility
> *That whorespondent is such a dumb whore she thinks Maria Menounos is a ship Columbus sailed on.*

wreckdum sex [*rek-dum sex*] noun
any type of intimate relations in which an individual ruins themselves, their partner, and/or their surroundings due to hygiene or behavior
> *Rosa thought she stumbled upon a crime scene when she saw the ruined bedspread and ripped out weave, but when the toothless skank came out of the bathroom, she knew it was a simple case of motel wreckdum sex.*

Thanxoxo for Sucking Less!

ACKNOWLEDGMENTS

My drama teacher, AMY WARMAN, for not questioning my bronzer usage or nipple rings when I turned Joseph in *Joseph and the Amazing Technicolor Dreamcoat* into a goddamn Pride parade.

ANTHONY TORREZ (aka Swag Coach at Large, aka DJ Pastabody, aka the Playlist Pimp), the closest thing I'll ever have to a brother. This book couldn't have happened without you, and you're entitled to one (1) free copy. He would also hate me if I didn't mention his Instagram Atorrez1. Take a letter, Maria. You're the best. I'm the worst.

MY AUNTS: (a) AUNT TINA for coming to my First Holy Communion in spandex shorts with a ripped jean overlay and with the best frosted blond hair, and for letting my best friend and me crash in your basement; (b and c) AUNT NANCY for always letting me watch shit on TV my parents wouldn't allow and for having dope girlfriends like Aunt DJ; (d) AUNT DONNA for being the first person to call me a faggot while fistfighting at a funeral after-party (my family is fun); and (e) AUNT MARY LOU for being classy as fuck and a role model. (I was doing this alphabetically and aunts count as *a*'s, but I can't deal with this alphabet shit anymore.)

RYAN MURPHY for being the first person to take me seriously and telling me a life-changing story about a shortie robe and Bill Condon.

DESIREE WEBBER for giving me a job when I was twelve so I could make enough money to escape central Florida.

PAULA ELLER for being a great broad and early sounding board. You're missed.

MY FAMILY: DAD for teaching me to be an asset in any situation I'm in, MOM for mouth, and SAM for teaching me how not to get caught at things. A shout-out to my Make-A-Wish sister, DANASHIYA! Hey, girl, hey.

My editor, DANA HAMILTON, for finding me, pitching me, and selling my book. You've showed me that I have a future as long as there's spell-check. Thank you to Hachette for the opportunity. ALL MY PAST REPS: TODD JUSTICE, DRAGON TALENT, MARC GERALD, and MAHZAD BABAYAN.

THE LADIES OF DEEP STEALTH: ANDREA, my editrix, for being the sharpest and most tactial tool in the shed, and my right hand lady, CALPERNIA, for the graphic design.

THE GAME SHOW FAM: Logo, Viacom, and all subsidiaries in perpetuity; DAVID CHARPENTIER for the gigs; SHANNON CALLAGHAN for telling me to shut up when I -need to; CHANEL PERILLO for making me stay past episode 2; MICHELLE VISAGE; BLAKE JACOBS; SWAGA DEB; CHRIS McKIM for calling me a "cancer" and without even knowing I was born in June; JACOB ISENBERGER; PAM POST; JEN STANDER and STEVEN CORFE for going over and above the call of duty; JASON SHUMAKER; JAKE SLANE; CARLY UDSIN; that production assistant whose name I forget but who fingered me; BILLY B; CHARLES RUNNETTE; DANIEL FRANZESE and BERT V. ROYAL; JAMES LAROSA (well, your show is Viacom anyway, so, hi); and HECTOR POCASANGRE.

ALL THE PEOPLE WHO HELPED ME BE PRETTY FOR THIS BOOK: @JamestheGemini on hair provided by MyWigsAndWeaves.com, BobbiePinz.com, and WigsByVanity.com; Sharon at Dr. Berkley's; Deann at Dr. Rosenblatt's; Nikita, my Pilates guru; Michael at Physical Therapy Care in Inglewood; Marco Marco and Chris Psaila; Scott Barnes and Frank Galasso; The Lady Hyde, aka Dallas Coulter; Delta Work; Ashton Michael; Richard Simmons; Johnny Wujek; Danny Dax; Lipstick Nick; Sean Harris; B. Calla; Pinky's Nails; @Tres_She; @Jeffyeffingt; @Dickallday; @Omgharleymadden; @Danielxmiller; and my girlfriend Amy.

CHRIS D'ARENZIO and KRISTIN HANGGI for helping me discover me through '80s rock and hairography.

ROBIN ROEMER for making me look like a pro. DAVID PHELPS, DEVINOGRAPHY, SHAUN VADELLA, PAUL BOULON, SHARLENE DURFEY, MAGNUS HASTINGS, and DUSTI CUNNINGHAM for additional photography. GINA GARAN and JACKIE CARLSON for giving me my writer's retreat.

ACKNOWLEDGMENTS

The people who taught me how to party at Tony 'n' Tina's Wedding before I got shitcanned: JOSH LAMON, DAWNE-MARRIE, LISA, ANNA, LAURA, RALPH, CAPRICE, AUNT GINNY, STEVE CARR, and ART.

ANTHONY LOPEZ, MOMMA, MADISON, ALEXIS ARQUETTE, MISS ALANNA, TRANZK, and all the CLUB MAKEUP kids.

DAVID and NEIL for letting my shartistry into your world and being all around awesome people.

DAVID KLASFELD and my OCC family: NICKY, JACK, THE HERRERA'S, BANJ, NATASHA, NICHOLE, JANUARY, and COURTNEY.

The specialest thank you to MATHU ANDERSEN for letting the world know it's OK to judge a book by its cover—especially the back one. You make the world a more beautiful place and inspire me daily.

NICOLE SARKIOGLU—OMG I wrote a book and you're in it! Hi!

BBB. Good game :)

RUPAUL. I owe you a lot for giving me my biggest break and changing my life.
    (I'm gonna write the rest normally since I don't think this'll exactly make his book list.)
    I can't thank him enough. Literally—I cannot thank him at all actually. The last time I saw him, I waved and yelled "hey Champ" from 10 feet away and he looked right through me and rode off on his bike. Family's don't always get along but I'm a Ru girl, goddammit, and that's

because Ru saw something in me and put my picture on that wall for season 4. First, too, from what casting said.

Ru has inspired me to be me from as far back as sixth grade. In his first book, he wrote about an incident at the MTV VMAs when he famously stood up for himself against Milton Berle's bullshit. He spoke up and was vilified for it. I've tried my best to follow in his footsteps and to not let people walk all over me. Hell, I try to make sure no one gets unfairly treated, and that has made ru-lations strained. My favorite quote is "Evil prevails when good men do nothing." Anyone who saw my meaty tuck in the Marco Marco show in 2016 knows I have balls and I'm not afraid to put my money where my mouth is (especially if there's money near balls). Anyway, the point is, I had one shining North Star growing up, and that was Ru. All a kid needs is one example. Who knows what would've happened had I not shoplifted RuPaul's cassette in 1993? Ru

was that hooker next to the Yellow Brick Road who demonstrated that It Gets Better is a LIE and I was gonna have to work my ass off. When I finally did make it to OZ, I was even more thankful for her but knew that I'd rather go back out on my own to a world with less smoke and mirrors. Gratitude should never be conditional though. It's like Dorothy smackin the shit outta Glinda for bamboozling her. It's about the journey. Do you guys get what I'm saying? If not, it's cool 'cause the book's almost over anyway. But yea. I hope, much like a Ru-know-who did for me, that I can bestow my messiest blessings on you and help everything to suck less.

ABOUT THE AUTHOR

Willam's cross-dress-for-success formula has made him relevant enough that he gets to write this bio in third person like an asshole. He graduated at the top of his class at sixteen after completing high school in three years. It remains one of the few things he's ever topped other than the Billboard Comedy Album chart with his number-one album *Shartistry in Motion*. Being the only contestant disqualified from *RuPaul's Drag Race* didn't stop him from becoming a model, actress, mattress, MTV host, and American Apparel ad girl, despite wearing as little clothing as possible and not being an actual girl. Internationally, he's followed in the steps of many iconic women by starring in the Cannes Film Festival's Golden Lion–winning Magnum campaign, overcoming both lactose intolerance and the fact that he's (again) not a girl. Cyberbullying and parody songs have garnered his YouTube channel more than 100 million views, and performances in more than 30 countries have found him evading arrest in Dubai on moral crimes and accidentally drug-muling in Singapore. Willam realizes that if hell exists, he will probably end up there, but hopefully his slacktivist work with various LA charities will offset his karmic offenses and he'll get a cute table with bottle service. If this book was printed on recycled paper, please know that Willam did not authorize it. For booking info, have your dad call his dad or go to WillamBelli. com. If this is a medical emergency, please hang up and dial 911.

Learn more at:
    WillamBelli.com
    Twitter: @Willam
    Facebook.com/willam
    Instagram: @willam
    YouTube.com/noextrai

Photo by Mathu Andersen

Living
with
Change

Positive Techniques for Transforming Your Life

Ursula Markham

First published by Element Books Ltd 1993
© Vega 2002
Text © Ursula Markham 1993

ISBN 1-84333-600-6

A catalogue record for this book is available
from the British Library

Published in 2002 by
Vega
64 Brewery Road
London, N7 9NT

A member of **Chrysalis** Books plc

Visit our website at www.chrysalisbooks.co.uk

Cover design, Grade Design Consultants, London
Printed in Great Britain by CPD, Wales